P9-EEG-996

Residential Crime

This project was supported by the
Law Enforcement Assistance Administration,
U.S. Department of Justice, under the
Omnibus Crime Control and Safe Streets
Act of 1968, as amended. Points of view
or opinions stated in this document are
those of the author and do not neces-
sarily represent the official position
or policies of the U.S. Department of
Justice.

Residential Crime

Thomas A. Reppetto

Ballinger Publishing Company • Cambridge, Mass.
A Subsidiary of J.B. Lippincott Company

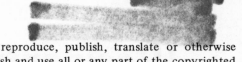

Prepared for Urban Systems Research & Engineering, Cambridge, Mass.

International Standard Book Number: 0-88410-209-2

Library of Congress Catalog Card Number: 74-12253

Printed in the United States of America

Library of Congress Cataloging in Publication Data

Reppetto, Thomas A
Residential Crime

    Bibliography: p.
    1. Burglary—Boston metropolitan area. 2. Robbery—Boston metropolitan area. 3. Victims of crimes—Boston metropolitan area. 4. Dwellings—Security measures. I. Title.
HV6661.M4R46   364'.9744'61   74-12253
ISBN 0-88410-209-2

Contents

List of Figures

List of Tables

Foreword

There is slowly arising a "new criminology" to supplement traditional criminology. To a large extent, crime has traditionally been studied from the point of view of the criminal (trying to discover what "causes" him or her to commit illegal acts), in ways that treat crime as a general and undifferentiated phenomenon (for example, any kind of "juvenile delinquency," or all the components of the FBI Crime Index), and with only limited concern for specific policies that might be effective in reducing crime. There are of course conspicuous exceptions—one thinks of Marvin Wolfgang's study of murder—but the prevailing pattern has been based on an intellectual orientation toward describing the incidence or explaining the causes of generalized forms of social deviance.

The new criminology—not literally new, of course, for there has always been some work in this vein—considers crime from the point of view of the victim, treats particular kinds of offenses (e.g., residential burglaries, stranger-to-stranger assaults), and considers explicitly the effectiveness of alternative prevention strategies. This book by Thomas A. Reppetto is a good example of the new criminology.

Reppetto, a former Commander in the Detective Division of the Chicago Police Department who went on to receive a doctorate in public administration at Harvard, considers in this study residential burglaries and robberies in the Boston metropolitan area. It is a study of a quite specific, albeit quite common, form of criminality in a particular setting—the home. Its focus is even more specific than simply burglaries, however, for in the course of the investigation it became clear that residential burglary was a very different crime depending on whether it was committed in a low-income public housing project in the central city or in a middle-class white suburb—so much so that deterrence strategies that might be appropriate for the former would be quite useless for the latter.

In method as well as focus this book shows some of the advances that have occurred in criminology in recent years. Not only are all official reports of these crimes studied, but interviews are carried out with a large number of victims and nonvictims and with nearly one hundred convicted burglars. In addition, the premises on which burglaries and robberies occurred were inspected to evaluate the implications for victimization of physical location and housing structure.

By focussing on the offense rather than the offender or the police, Reppetto avoids the common pitfall of "overexplaining" crime. Studies that examine offenders tend to find so many factors that apparently contribute to the proclivity to steal—poverty, low education, youthful bravado, relative deprivation, social isolation, peer-group influences, family disorganization, habitual drug abuse, and so on—that crime seems impossible to prevent except by massive (and unlikely) social transformations. Furthermore, such offender-oriented studies explain neither why some persons exposed to the same social forces that lead others to crime are not themselves led to it nor why even crime-prone persons commit offenses in some places and at some times but not in other places or at other times.

By evaluating not only the outlook of the offender but the physical circumstances of each offense—ease of access, frequency of police patrols, availability of loot, proximity to the burglar's own residence, social composition of the neighborhood—Reppetto is able to place the residential burglary in its full context in a way that suggests how criminal motivation interacts with opportunity to produce a particular pattern of burglary that varies in predictable ways and thus perhaps in ways that can be deliberately altered.

The reader will find in this book a reconsideration of Oscar Newman's famous argument about "defensible space," some startling findings about the relationship between weapons and personal injury in robberies, and more depressing facts about the inadequacy of the judicial response to the criminality. It is the kind of book that ought to stimulate imitation; that would be the most useful form of flattery.

James Q. Wilson

Acknowledgments

This study of the patterns of residential crime was carried on under the auspices of the National Institute of Law Enforcement and Criminal Justice (NILECJ), Law Enforcement Assistance Administration (LEAA), United States Department of Justice, and the Department of Housing and Urban Development (DHUD). I wish to acknowledge my debt to these agencies and particularly to Dr. Fred Heinzelmann, Dr. Michael Maltz, Dr. Richard Rav, Mr. George Schollenberger, of NILECJ, and Mr. John Dietrich of the Office of Science and Technology of DHUD.

Acknowledgment is also made to former Commissioner Edmund McNamara, Deputy Superintendent John Bonner and Sergeant William Bulger of the Boston Police Department, Chief William Quinn, and Officer John Roman of the Newton Police Department and the late Chief James Murphy and Chief Clerk Albert Bishop of the Norwood Police Department, for their cooperation and assistance in gathering crime data.

I am also grateful to Mr. Peter Borre, former Director of the Mayors Safe Streets Act Committee, City of Boston, and his associate Ms. Deborah Blumin as well as Mr. Leo Gulinello, Director of Security for the Boston Housing Authority for their assistance in gathering additional crime data.

I am further indebted to Commissioner C. Elliot Sands of the Massachusetts Department of Probation, Sheriff John Buckley of Middlesex County, and Mr. Richard Doucette, Master of the County House of Correction, Mr. Joseph McBrine, former Commissioner of the Suffolk County (Boston) House of Correction, Chief Probation Officer Matthew Connolly of the Dorchester District Court and Mr. Donald Stevens, Probation Officer of the Brighton District Court for their assistance in locating offenders to interview.

The survey research aspects of the project were carried on under the supervision of Dr. Floyd Fowler, Director of the Survey Research Program of the Harvard-MIT Joint Center for Urban Studies and the University of Massachusetts. Dr. Fowler was assisted by Ms. Molly McCalla and Mrs. Alice Fehlhaber.

For their helpful comments I am also indebted to Mr. Arnold Sagalyn, Mr. George Van de Mark, Mr. John Labovitz, Mr. Peter Labovitz, and Mr. John Williams of the Security Planning Corporation of Washington, D.C.

Staff for the original study was provided by Urban Systems Research and Engineering Inc. of Cambridge, Massachusetts, under the direction of Dr. Anthony J. Blackburn, President of USR&E. The literature search was conducted by Ms. Carol Hoffman and Ms. Mary Morton. Ms. Ellen Mason was principal analyst for the household survey data pertaining to victims and nonvictims; Ms. Christa Carnegie performed a similar function relating to structural victimization. Ms. Jane Dedman was responsible for the site survey phase of the project and was research assistant to the author. The offender interviews were carried on under the direction of Ms. Joanna Breyer with the assistance of Dr. Barry Sacks, Mr. Charles Sabatelle, and Mr. John Cooper, along with Ms. Morton, Ms. Hoffman, Ms. Dedman, and Ms. Carnegie. Mr. Clark Binkley supervised the quantitative data analysis. This manuscript originally comprised two volumes. Its conversion from a large technical report to the present format is largely the work of Ms. Stephanie Gould, assisted by Ms. Joan Nelson.

I am indebted for incisive comments and criticisms provided by Dr. Harrison White, Professor of Sociology at Harvard University, and Dr. Gary Marx, Professor of Urban Studies and Planning at MIT.

Thomas A. Reppetto

Residential Crime

CHAPTER ONE

Introduction

BACKGROUND

This study of residential robberies and burglaries originated in an atmosphere of growing concern over what the popular press has come to call "America's spiralling crime rate." Substantial evidence (the present study included) indicates that this phrase is no mere journalistic cliche. In 1972, for example, the FBI Uniform Crime Reports noted a 59 percent increase in the *rate* at which "violent"[a] crimes were committed from 1967 to 1972 and a 45 percent increase in the rate for crimes against property.[b][1] Although much debate has centered on the question of whether these increases are actual or only a product of improved reporting procedures, the concensus (enunciated by the President's Commission on Violence, among others) seems to be that, in spite of the numerous reporting problems, significant increases in the "true" rates for both crimes of violence and crimes against property have occurred over the past several years.[2] And, statistical questions aside, the increase in public concern about crime is incontestable.

> To millions of Americans few things are more pervasive, more frightening, more real today than violent crime and the fear of being assaulted, mugged, robbed, or raped. The fear of being victimized by criminal attack has touched us all in some way. People are fleeing their residences in cities to the expected safety of suburban living. Residents of many areas will not go out on the street at night. Others have added bars and extra locks to windows and doors in their homes.[3]

---

[a]Murder, forcible rape, robbery, aggravated assault.
[b]Burglary, larceny $50.00 and over, and auto theft.

1

Here then, are two distinct causes for concern: rising crime rates and a rising level of public fear. Although obviously interrelated, the two phenomena operate in some respects independently of one another: particularly in that, while public fear focuses on the criminal "stranger," the violent crimes (murder, rape, assault) which inspire the greatest fear in fact occur relatively rarely between strangers. A Philadelphia study found, for example, that only 12 percent of all homicides occurring over a four-year period involved persons who were unacquainted with one another.[4] Similarly, the President's Commission on Crime in the District of Columbia found that only one third of a sample of rape victims and 19 percent of aggravated assault victims were attacked by strangers.[5]

These findings, which are buttressed by various other studies, as well as by the Uniform Crime Reports, suggest the dilemma of the criminologist in attempting to strategize against "crime" as an undifferentiated phenomenon. Obviously, for example, crimes of violence occurring among friends constitute a different sort of social problem than does, say auto theft—and also constitute a problem which the criminal justice system is ill-equipped to counter. Thus, although the public may fear a generalized "crime wave," those concerned with crime prevention must distinguish among different types of crimes, committed by different criminals in different ways for different reasons. Such realizations underlie the increasingly crime-specific orientation of modern criminological research.

The present study, which was conducted in the Boston Metropolitan Area, carries this trend one step further in focusing not only on specific crimes but on specific environments for the commission of these crimes. The particular crimes of concern—residential burglary and robbery—were selected for study because (1) they are primarily stranger to stranger (2) of all environments in which stranger-to-stranger crimes can occur, the "home"—now become a sanctuary from the perils of the street—is potentially the most threatening and (3) of all serious stranger-to-stranger crimes which do occur on residential premises, burglary and robbery are by far the most common. In fact, robbery and burglary are the only crimes which are commonly classified as "residential" in character; for in general, criminal law, crime statistics and criminological research are not organized around a concept of crime "locales." In defining the crime of rape, for example, the law requires no specification of locale, the Uniform Crime Reports do not contain a category of residential rape, and studies of criminal histories of rapists do not single out those who might choose to attack exclusively or primarily strangers on residential premises. Likewise, other offenses rarely occur on residential premises between strangers (murder, assault), or seldom occur in the home (larceny),[6] or are not usually serious (vandalism). (Appendix A contains a discussion of the percentage of various crimes in the Boston area which fall into the 'residential' classification.)

RESIDENTIAL ROBBERY AND BURGLARY

Robbery and burglary, then, differ from most other serious crimes in that they generally occur between strangers and relatively frequently occur within or around the home. Robbery is the stealing or taking of anything of value from a person by force, violence, or putting in fear. If it occurs on residential premises, it is classified as residential robbery, which, according to Boston police records, constitutes 10 percent of all robberies. Much of the so-called residential robbery, however, does not involve direct intrusion into dwellings, but more typically the victim (often a nonresident) is attacked in an adjacent area, such as a hallway. In some respects, these crimes tend to resemble street robbery, and the fact that they occur on residential premises may often be a matter of chance. Other residential robberies may begin as burglaries, but because of an unexpected encounter between offender and victim, they become robberies.

The prototype of residential crime is the offense of burglary. In its original common law definition, burglary involved the breaking and entering of the dwelling unit of another at night with the intent to commit a felony.[7] This definition encompasses all the elements that the public tends to associate with residential crime—forcible entry into a dwelling at a time when the occupants are expected to be home, for the purpose of committing a serious offense. At present in the United States, however, under UCR definition and often by state statute, the offense of burglary can be committed against non-dwelling structures, can occur at any time of the day, and does not require a forcible entry. Indeed, nearly half of the burglaries reported annually do not take place in dwellings,[c] and the overwhelming number of residential burglaries are committed at a time when the occupants are away.

Not only do robberies and burglaries occur relatively frequently in comparison with other crimes between strangers on residential premises; in addition, the rate at which these crimes are committed appears to be increasing substantially, for both the nation as a whole and for the Boston Metropolitan Area. Between 1966 and 1970, for example, reported residential burglary in Boston increased 150 percent and reported residential robbery, 400 percent. Table 1-1 documents this increase. Since the President's Crime Commission estimated in 1966 that approximately half of all robberies and two thirds of all burglaries went unreported, and since subsequent victimization studies (including one conducted for this project) have continued to find much unreported crime, the increases reflected in Table 1-1 would not appear solely attributable to improved reporting procedures.

---

[c]In 1970, the UCR listed 58 percent of all reported burglaries as residential; however, some of these occurred in unattached garages or on other nondwelling property. See FBI, *UCR, 1970,* p. 21.

Table 1-1.   Residential Robbery and Burglary Rates per 100,000 Population

Category		1962	1966	1970
Residential	U. S.A.	207	343[b]	614
Burglary	Boston	248[a]	434	1089
Residential	U.S.A.	4	6[b]	21
Robbery	Boston	5[a]	13	51

[a]Estimate based on population of 675,000
[b]Estimate based on population of 650,000
Source: FBI *UCR* 1962, 1966, 1970
    Annual Reports Boston Police Department 1962, 1966, 1970.

Also, FBI statistics for 1972 indicate that residential robberies and burglaries have been increasing at a faster rate than the nonresidential versions of these crimes. Residential robbery, for example, increased by 105 percent from 1967-1972, while the overall robbery rate (which includes commercial, bank, and street robberies as well as residential) increased by 85 percent. During the same period, residential burglary rose by approximately 73 percent, compared with a 46 percent increase in the overall burglary rate (residential and nonresidential).[8] Reasons for the more rapid growth of residential crimes would be very hard to come by and harder still to document, but one can nevertheless hypothesize that this growth may continue and, indeed, become even more pronounced as more and more commercial enterprises avail themselves of increasingly sophisticated security devices and techniques. In other words, the growth of residential "theft crimes" may possibly be anticipated as a kind of displacement effect of the elaborate security measures more readily available to businesses than to individuals.

Whether or not this problematic development occurs, the consequences of the *present* level of residential robberies and burglaries are sufficiently severe to merit isolating these crimes for individual study. Although the average losses from residential burglary and robbery are relatively small ($330 for the former, $268 for the latter), the gross losses for burglary are substantial: approximately $465 million annually.[9] And, if the number of unreported residential burglaries were taken into account, the total loss could be estimated in the vicinity of one billion dollars. Of course, there are also indirect economic costs— insurance, locks, alarm devices, etc.—but all these economic costs taken together are far overshadowed by the personal and social consequences of these crimes.

Although burglary, by definition, is not a crime of force or threat, what begins as a burglary may end up as a robbery—and robbery, by definition, does involve a fear-producing confrontation. The President's Crime Commission estimated that approximately 1 in 40 burglaries results in sufficient confrontation to reclassify it as a robbery,[10] but data gathered for the present study indicated that 1 in 100 would be a more accurate estimate.[d] Other data on residential robberies indicated that approximately half of these crimes involve physical attacks upon the victims.[11] Projections from these study figures show that, for example, in a city of 640,000, 150-200 persons would be assaulted annually in the course of residential robberies—which is less than one victim per 3,000 population.

The relative rarity with which either residential robbery or burglary results in personal injury is not, however, an adequate measure of the personal and social consequences of these crimes. By far the most pervasive consequence— fear—is not readily susceptible to statistical summation, but its influence is obvious. The minifortresses—housing for the affluent—springing up around the central cities, the growth of neighborhood patrol groups, the flight of the middle class to the suburbs, the flourishing security business—all testify to the penetration of fear into the most private of places: the home.

The present study, then, is a product of the concern felt by the Law Enforcement Assistance Administration (LEAA) and the Department of Housing and Urban Development (HUD) over the growing problem of residential crime. The study, which represents the first phase of a multiphase project, was undertaken to determine the nature and pattern of common crimes committed in and around residential properties in both urban and suburban areas. Rather than probing any one component of the crime problem in great depth, the study sought to provide a broad picture of the two most common residential crimes through examination of the three major elements which interact in the occur- rence of any crime: the offender, his environment, and his victim. The ultimate end of the entire project is, of course, the design of more effective control strategies for residential crimes.

METHODOLOGY

Toward the end of establishing more effective control strategies for residential burglaries and robberies, this study sought to identify, describe, and, where possible, explain in a systematic and quantitative manner the rates and patterns

---

[d]The commission apparently assumed all residential robberies begin as burg- laries. An analysis of 152 residential robberies in Boston during 1969-1971 determined that only one third took place in the dwelling unit. The rest were in hallways, elevators, etc., where the offender's presence was not necessarily unlawful (i.e., burglarious). Of those in the dwelling unit, it is not always possible to determine the offender's state of mind when he committed the crime. In several instances a ruse was used to gain entrance, indicating that the offender knew the premises were occupied and he was going to engage in a robbery. Even if it were assumed that all cases within the dwelling where the offender's intentions were unclear were actually burglaries that turned into robberies, this would constitute only 25 percent of all residential robberies in the sample. Projecting these figures citywide, it would mean that no more than one burglary in 90 turns into a robbery. Clearly, 1/100 is much closer to reality than one in 40.

of these crimes and their correlation to key variables. "Rates" are defined as the number of offenses per unit (generally measured in crimes per 1,000 households per year); "patterns" are the chronological and spatial distribution of rates and the distinctive characteristics of methods and target choices; and "correlative factors" are social and physical circumstances which appear to relate to, and possibly explain, the rates and patterns.

The information used in the study was obtained from:

1. a search of the literature, both popular and academic;
2. an anlysis of criminal justice system records pertaining to residential crime, including a close examination of 2,500 murders, rapes, robberies, and burglaries;
3. a survey of households which included both a detailed interview with nearly 1,000 victims and nonvictims of residential robberies and burglaries and an audit of the security aspects of their dwelling units;
4. a field observation study of the comparative security features of 39 selected geographic areas;
5. a study of residential offender behavior, including detailed interviews with and an analysis of the criminal history of 97 adjudicated burglars.

The site selected for the study, the metropolitan Boston area, was assumed to possess a residential crime problem more or less typical of urban areas throughout the country. (This assumption was made in the absence of any indication to the contrary and under the necessity of limiting the data to a workable scope. Where possible and relevant, information from studies of other areas is used to evaluate the data for Boston.) No attempt was made to provide an exhaustive account of residential robbery and burglary in the Boston area. Rather, 39 "representative" areas of the Boston Standard Metropolitan Statistical Area were selected according to a stratification of housing type, race, income, and crime rate, as follows:

Housing Type
    Public housing
    Large multiunit dwellings
    Small multiunit dwellings
    Single family dwellings
Race
    Predominantly white
    Predominantly black
    Mixed
Income
    Low
    Medium
    High

Crime
  Low reported residential burglary rate
  Medium reported residential burglary rate
  High reported residential burglary rate

      Thirty-six of the thirty-nine areas are in the city of Boston proper, where each comprises one of the city's 824 police reporting areas, commonly called RAs.[e] (See Appendix A(2), Figure A(2)-1) The RAs are the smallest subdivision for which crime records are kept. The next largest unit of crime recording is the neighborhood, of which there are 81 in Boston. The neighborhoods generally comprise coherent social, economic, and geographic communities. Neighborhoods are grouped into twelve police districts,[f] which roughly correspond to the historic divisions of Boston as they were incorporated into the city proper and are the present administrative subdivisions of the city police department (see Appendix A(2), Figure A(2)-2).

      A district, therefore is a group of neighborhoods and a neighborhood is a group of RAs. Within this report the terms area, neighborhood, and district will refer to the units described above.

      Since suburban police do not use the reporting area concept, the suburban areas under study are actually census tracts for which crime data was especially collected for this project (see Appendix A(2), Figure A(2)-3). Appendix A(3), Table A(3)-1, identifies all the studied areas by neighborhood and police district.

      After the 39 representative areas were selected, police records were gathered and analyzed for all residential robberies ($N = 152$) and burglaries ($N = 1988$) reported in each area between 1/1/69 and 9/30/71.[g] Concurrent with this phase of the project detailed interviews were conducted with 97 adjudicated residential burglars.

      Next, from the original 39 areas, 18 were selected for further analysis from within the stratified categories (see Appendix A, Figures A(2)-1 and A(2)-3). This took the form of a household survey of nearly 1,000 victims and nonvictims and a site survey of the environment.

      Throughout the rest of the book, data from the victimization survey conducted for this project is used as a check on police records, since numerous other studies have already indicated that a significant amount of crime is—for various reasons—never reflected in official statistics. Indeed, a 1970 survey of the Boston area showed a residential burglary rate almost triple that

---

[e]Three areas 196, 470, and 745 are actually two RAs combined into one.

[f]Two districts were recently combined, but for crime analysis purposes the city continues to use the 12-district framework.

[g]City police data for the last three months of 1971 was not available at the time of the records search. Suburban police data was available only for 1970 and 1971.

recorded in official police statistics. The disparity is shown in Table 1-2:

Table 1–2 Comparison of Official and Unofficial Residential Burglary Rates—Boston, 1970

	Per 1000 Households
Official rate[a]	32
Survey rate[b]	120

[a]See report of the Police Commissioner, City of Boston, 1970, Table IV.
[b]Fowler, Floyd, *Report on Citizen Attitudes Toward City Services in Ten Cities,* Harvard-MIT Joint Center for Urban Studies (to be published).

This finding parallels the Presidential Commission report noted earlier and was generally duplicated in nine other cities which underwent similar surveys as part of a national study.[12]

While the problem of unreported crime is known to researchers, the prevailing view has been that:

> It is not necessary to know about every act that occurs. Official information would still be adequate for most crimes to show the relative variation in crime rate in different city areas, providing that the offenses and the offenders in these areas have roughly the same chance of coming to official notice and action. There is increasing evidence . . . that this assumption is probably true, especially for the more serious offenses which are not confined in the family context.[13]

As expected from such previous surveys, all RAs included in the present survey reported more offenses than police figures indicated. However, in two officially low rate RAs the survey uncovered an amount of unreported burglary sufficient to raise doubts concerning the relative variation between areas in actual and reported crime figures,[h] and recent independent victimization study of one of the two areas (196) reported annual burglary rates in excess of 500/1000 households.[14] These findings necessitated great circumspection in the use of police data for this project, so whenever feasible, the data was evaluated in conjunction with information obtained from other sources.

---

[h]In RA 196, the recorded rate for the first nine months of 1971 was 3/1000. Yet, from a total of 43 supposedly nonvictimized households interviewed, six burglaries were sustained in the same time period. In RA 447 the official rate for the first nine months of 1971 was 10/1000, but of 68 nonvictim households surveyed, ten sustained burglaries during that period. In later sections of the present study, the analysis will frequently find 196 and 447 standing out from their group. It is likely, therefore, that these are not low burglary rate areas.

The remainder of this book presents research both under separate topics and as an integrated whole. Chapter 2 discusses the behavior patterns of residential burglars and robbers; Chapter 3, how these patterns may be influenced by the socioeconomic and physical characteristics of the environment in which the offenders operate; and Chapter 4, the characteristics of the houses and persons "victimized" by these offenders. Chapter 5 then presents the current methods and theories for control of residential robbery and burglary and outlines the implications of this study for future control strategies.

NOTES

1. FBI, *Uniform Crime Reports 1972* (Washington, D.C.: U.S. Government Printing Office, 1973): Charts 2 and 3, pp. 4, 5.

2. National Commission on the Causes and Prevention of Violence—Task Force on Individual Acts of Violence, *Crimes of Violence* (Washington, D.C.: U.S. Government Printing Office, 1969): Vol. 11, pp. xxvii, 49, 50.

3. Ibid, p. xxv.

4. Marvin E. Wolfgang, *Patterns of Criminal Homicide* (Philadelphia: University of Pennsylvania Press, 1958).

5. *Report of the President's Commission on Crime in the District of Columbia* (Washington, D.C.: U.S. Government Printing Office, 1966): 53.

6. Op. cit. *UCR 1972* (Washington, D.C.: U.S. Government Printing Office, 1971): Table 22 and op. cit. *Crimes of Violence* 221.

7. See *Black's Law Dictionary,* Revised 4th edition (St. Paul: West Publishing Company, 1968): 247.

8. Op. cit., *UCR 1972*: 17, 20.

9. Op. cit., *UCR 1972* 21.

10. President's Commission on Law Enforcement and Administration of Justice, *Task Force Report: Crime and its Impact—An Assessment* (Washington, D.C.: U.S. Government Printing Office, 1967): 15; FBI, *Uniform Crime Reports 1965* (Washington, D.C.: U.S. Government Printing Office, 1966): Table 14, p. 105.

11. See Chapter 2.

12. Floyd Fowler, *Report on Citizen Attitudes Toward City Services in Ten Cities,* Harvard-M.I.T. Joint Center for Urban Studies (to be published).

13. Op. cit., *Crime and Its Impact*: 64.

14. Deborah Blumin, *Victims: A Study of Crime in a Boston Housing Project* (Boston: Mayor's Office of Justice Administration, 1973).

Chapter Two

Offender Behavior

BACKGROUND

Criminal offender typologies are usually constructed according to categories of target or motivation (property, person, sex offender, etc.) or legal definitions (robber, burglar, rapist) rather than in terms of location of offense (residence, street, commercial establishment), which makes their applicability to residential crimes rather tenuous. Nevertheless, a brief review of previous research on offender behavior will provide some necessary perspective for the present study.

For the general class of property offenders (robbers as well as burglars and thieves), Gibbons and Garrity[1] offer a typology which assumes that the real world of criminal behavior is comprised of social roles or stable behavior patterns and that these role patterns are differentiated along two major dimensions: self-definition and attitudes, and offense behavior, of which the latter is of primary concern for the present purposes. As regards offense behavior, they differentiate a so-called professional or "heavy" from the nonprofessional property offender—the former being characterized by a high degree of technical skill and large profit in the operations he undertakes, and the latter by lack of planning, lack of skills, and meager profit.

Clinnard and Quinney also associate "professionalism" with a high level of skill, but they specifically exclude the typical robber and burglar from this classification. The nonviolent confidence man is cited as the archtypical professional, and most robbers and burglars are—because of their unprofessional disposition toward violence—labelled as merely "conventional," a class of criminal which occupies the ". . . bottom of the scale of career crime." While the professional is characterized by a high level of skill in his operations, the conventional criminal is "less skillful in committing offenses and not as well organized to avoid arrest and conviction."[2]

On the other hand, a group of researchers working on a pilot study for the President's Crime Commission[3] did not equate 'professional' with skillful and, instead, defined professional crime as "crime committed for personal or economic gain by individuals whose major source of income is from criminal pursuits and who spend the majority of their working time in illegal enterprises." This definition excluded organized and white collar crime and concentrated mainly on predatory offenses (such as robbery or burglary) involving a unwilling victim. The Commission researchers did, however, differentiate between high and medium and low status professional criminals and consigned to the class "high status" many of the characteristics which other criminologists have ascribed to "professionals." That is, the high status criminals engaged in a great deal of planning, expected loyalty from their associates, and tended to be specialized.

It appears, then, that the debate over skill classifications may be largely irrelevant to a discussion of residential robbers and burglars, who—regardless, of class labels—are generally characterized as having only limited skills, doing little planning, and obtaining relatively modest profits from their work. Although existing literature does suggest numerous possible differences in attitudes and motivation among residential criminals, these differences lie outside the scope of the present study, which concentrates primarily on behavioral—"operational"—characteristics rather than on "psychological" ones.

However, the observations on skills, planning, and profits mentioned above are generally confirmed in the remaining sections of this chapter, which is primarily intended to provide some basic understanding of the types of criminals who engage in residential crime and their common methods of operation.

RESIDENTIAL BURGLARS

The information used in the following analysis was obtained from police reports on 1,988 residential burglaries (the total number of such crimes reported over a 3-year period in the 39 reporting areas under study) and personal interviews with 97 adjudicated burglars. The interviews were conducted chiefly to obtain detailed information on how and why particular burglars attack particular dwellings, and the interviewees were—of necessity—all volunteers. Correctional officials prohibited any implication of coercion in the interview process, and, in any case, random sampling would undoubtedly have produced an unworkably large number of nonresponsive interviewees. (The interview procedure is described in detail in Appendix B.) Although the validity of the interview data is limited by the small size of the sample, possible biases from nonrandom selection and possible lack of veracity among the interviewees, these limitations were not considered sufficient to invalidate the restricted purpose for which the data was collected. Also, general behavioral similarities between the sample burglar population and the real world burglar population were established throughout the following analysis by comparison of interview data with police crime and arrest reports and data from a victimization survey of 1,000 households.

Demographic Characteristics

As anticipated by other studies and by FBI statistics, (see Table 2-1), persons arrested for burglary in Boston tend disproportionately to be young, male, and nonwhite.

Table 2–1: Demographic Characteristics of Persons Arrested for Burglary—1970

	Nationally[a]	*U.S. Cities*[b]	*U.S. Suburbs*[c]	*Boston*[d]
% Male	95%	95%	95%	97%
Median Age	17	17	17	18
% Nonwhite	4	39	18	45

Source: *FBI Uniform Crime Reports 1970*
[a]Tables 28, 30, 32.
[b]Cities are defined as municipalities with over 2500 population. Tables 34, 36, 38.
[c]Tables 40, 42, 43.
[d]Source: *Annual Report Police Commissioner for the City of Boston 1970,* Table VIII.

The population interviewed for this study was, in general, demographically similar to the arrested population, although somewhat older. Table 2-2 compares those interviewed with those arrested and with the Boston population as a whole.

Table 2–2: Demographic Characteristics of Persons Arrested for Burglary in Boston 1970, Compared to City Population and Interviewed Population

	Arrested Burglars	*Interviewed Population*	*City Population*
% Male	97%	100%	46%
Median Age	18	24	28.7
% Nonwhite	45%	46%	16%

As anticipated by the introduction to this chapter, classification of interviewees according to skill levels did not prove appropriate for our purposes, since almost all of the burglars interviewed for our study fell into the category of semiskilled. Also, as a group, the interviewees were not well educated and had limited noncriminal work skills; nearly 80 percent had never earned more than $200/week in a legitimate occupation, and nearly 60 percent were in jail at the time they were interviewed. A large percentage (83 percent) admitted to being involved previously in other illegal activities (principally auto theft and drug law violations) and to having also broken into nonresidential buildings, particularly stores and offices. Comparatively few (21 percent), however, admitted to having committed any robberies. (See also Appendix B, Tables B(2)-1 through B(2)-5).

A check of the interviewees' official criminal histories generally verified their own accounts, although some (understandably) failed to mention certain serious assaults with which they had been charged. On the other hand, several individuals admitted to crimes which, though consistent with their histories, did not appear in official records.

Pretesting did reveal behavioral differences between interviewees, but these differences appeared chiefly correlated to differences of age, race, and drug use rather than to differences in professional skill or previous criminal history. Accordingly, these three categories, subclassified as follows, form the typology by which the interviewed data is analyzed:

Age	*Race*	*Drug Use*
Under 18	White	Drug user
18–25	Nonwhite	Nondrug user
Over 25		

The overlap between the categories—most noticeable in the 18-25 age group, 68 percent of whom are drug users—is indicated in Table 2-3.

Table 2–3. Drug Use of Interviewees by Race and Age

	White		Nonwhite		
Age	*Drug user*	*Nondrug user*	*Drug user*	*Nondrug user*	*Total*
Under 18	1 (5%)	11 (52%)	4 (19%)	5 (24%)	21 (100%)
18–25	19 (37%)	5 (10%)	16 (31%)	11 (22%)	51 (100%)
Over 25	6 (24%)	10 (40%)	2 (8%)	7 (28%)	25 (100%)
Total	26	26	22	23	97

Target Selection

Interviewees were shown slide sequences of different types of housing and asked to select the type similar to that in which they most frequently operated and also to cite the reasons for their selections. The slides were photographs of actual buildings of the following types:

A public housing project with elevator buildings;
A group of attached (row) houses;
A group of small multifamily houses (known locally as three- or four-deckers);
A group of large multiunit older brick apartment buildings;
A group of luxury high-rise apartment buildings;
A group of single-family houses.

Table 2-4 indicates the selections of the interviewees and Table 2-5 the reasons offered for these selections. As is apparent from these tables, single-family houses were selected most often by the over-25 age group, most of whom indicated that apparent affluence was the prime factor in their choice of targets. The younger age group, on the other hand, generally selected housing projects and multifamily homes, and indicated that their choices were dictated much more by the accessibility of the structure than by the probability of substantial gain. Whites and drug users were also somewhat more likely to select the affluent single family homes than were nonwhites and nondrug users. Only the oldest group—again, valuing affluence—expressed any significant interest in luxury apartments; most of the interviewees in all categories indicated that the presence of security guards and elaborate protection devices rendered these structures relatively invulnerable to attack.

The aversion of the interviewees to luxury apartments was borne out by police and victimization survey data, which confirm that these structures have in fact the lowest victimization rate of any housing type. (See page 46.) Although single-family homes were selected by interviewed burglars more frequently than housing projects, the survey data presented in Table 2-6 indicates that housing projects have higher burglary rates than single-family homes. The apparent discrepancy between targets selected by interviewees and real-world victimization patterns parallels the bias of our sample toward older offenders and suggests that the real world burglar population is as young as the police records mentioned earlier indicate.

As a check on the expressed preferences, interviewees were also asked which housing types they would avoid and why. The results, which are presented in Appendix B, Tables B(2)-6 and B(2)-7, are generally consistent with those obtained for preferential housing types. The oldest group most generally avoided housing projects and indicated that they were most deterred by the likelihood of small profits, and seldom by police or security patrol. Younger burglars were least likely to work in single-family homes and luxury apartments and were most often deterred by the possibility of police or security patrols.

As regards differences in choice by racial factors, nonwhites were most likely to avoid single-family homes and whites, to avoid housing projects.

Table 2–4. What Housing Types Did Interviewees Most Frequently Operate in, in Total, by Age, Race, and Drug Use?

	Total	Age			Race		Drug Use	
		Under 18	18-25	Over 25	W	Non W	DU	Non DU
Single Family House	35%	14%	35%	52%	41%	29%	44%	27%
Multifamily House	28	33	33	12	26	29	21	35
Housing Project	19	33	18	8	12	28	12	24
Old brick apartment building	8	5	10	8	9	6	13	4
Row house	6	14	2	8	6	6	6	6
Luxury apartment	4	0	2	12	6	2	4	4
Total	97%	21%	51%	25%	52%	45%	48%	49%

Table 2–5. What Were the Main Reasons Interviewees Gave for Their Choices, in Total and by Age, Race, and Drug Use?

	Total	Age			Race		Drug Use	
		Under 18	18-25	Over 25	W	Non W	DU	Non DU
Ease of access	44%	52%	42%	40%	46%	42%	44%	45%
Appears affluent	41	24	40	56	46	36	46	37
Feels inconspicuous[a]	21	29	13	28	23	18	17	24
Isolated neighborhood	19	0	21	32	27	9	21	16
Few police security patrols	19	29	13	20	15	22	17	20
Neighbors don't know each other[b]	12	24	6	16	15	9	13	12
Total	97	21	51	25	52	45	48	49

Examples

[a]Fits into neighborhood—same race or age as residents.

[b]Either a transient, fast shifting neighborhood (students, working girls), or single family, possibly elderly neighborhood where houses isolated from each other.

**Table 2–6.   Residential Burglary
Victimization of Single-Family Houses
and Housing Projects**

	Rate Per 1000/D.U.
Single-family houses	94
Housing projects	103

Source: Household survey data.

Whites were also slightly more apt to avoid nonwhite neighborhoods in general, and nonwhites who avoided white neighborhoods tended to fall into the young and relatively inexperienced age group. Few differences emerged between the selections of drug users and nondrug users, although the nondrug users were somewhat more concerned about police patrols.

Analysis of police arrest data for specific locales highlights some of these patterns. For example, arrest records for one housing project area indicated no arrests of burglars over twenty-five. In contrast, 30 percent of the burglars arrested in a predominantly white apartment area were 25 or older. Only 7 percent of those arrested in a predominantly white suburban area were nonwhite, and only 16 percent of those arrested in a predominantly black inner-city area were white (see Appendix B, Table B(2)-8).

Method of Operation (Appendix B, Tables B(2)-9-12

Planning.   Approximately three quarters of the interviewees indicated that they engaged in some kind of planning, with the older burglars tending to do somewhat more planning and drug addicts and younger burglars somewhat less. All of the groups were primarily concerned (although drug addicts somewhat less concerned) with establishing whether or not the dwelling was occupied, since they much preferred to hit unoccupied residences.

Police data confirms the burglar's reluctance to confront the householder, since in 92 percent of the cases studies ($N = 1910$), the premises were unoccupied when the burglary occurred. Of the 82 cases where the premises were occupied and the occupants' state determined, in 51 percent of the cases the occupants were sleeping and in 14 percent the occupants—though awake—were unaware that burglaries were taking place. In the remaining 35 percent of the cases, the occupants were aware of the burglaries, but there was insufficient confrontation to cause the crimes to be reclassified as robberies.

Overall, the preference of the interviewees for unoccupied residences correlated with their preference for daytime over nightime work. Most interviewees worked in the morning (between 6 A.M. and 12 noon), and very few worked after midnight, when most people were likely to be home in bed. Again, this time preference is confirmed by police data; most reported burglaries occur during the day—and more often during the week than on the weekends. Only in housing projects and suburban areas was there a tendency for burglary to occur at night and on weekends.

Approximately, one third of all the interviewees wanted evidence of valuables on the premises (which they obtained from window peeping or on tips from friends) and one-third also wanted to know whether a burglar alarm system was in use. Few of the interviewees spent time assessing the frequency of police patrols, location of entrances or availability of escape routes although, again, the oldest group was most likely to be concerned with these matters. Probably as a result of their greater attention to planning, the oldest group was most confident about their ability to operate in well-protected neighborhoods and least likely to be deterred by police patrols or burglar alarms.

Transport.   Approximately one-half of the interviewees, mostly the young and nonwhite groups, indicated their unwillingness to travel more than one hour from their homes to make a hit. Since the younger and nonwhite groups were also most likely to travel on foot, they tended more than the other groups to operate within their own neighborhoods. The older age groups were willing to travel further afield (25 percent of the oldest groups were willing to travel more than 24 hours) and to use a car (the 18-25 group, stolen cars, and the over-25 group, their own cars).

The interviewees' responses tended on the whole to coincide with their criminal histories; nearly half showed a consistent pattern of arrests in the area in which they resided. Also, approximately half indicated their willingness to work in their own neighborhoods.

Methods (Appendix B, Tables B(2)-13-15).   Almost half the interviewees indicated that they always used at least one accomplice, whose usual function was that of a lookout man. The most consistent use of accomplices was found among the youngest age group—for whom breaking and entering was often a group activity—and among drug users. Only a fourth of the interviewees admitted to carrying any weapon (knife, gun, mace), and the most consistently carried tool for all categories of burglars was the simple screwdriver, followed by a crowbar.

The interviewees were more likely to employ these tools against doors than against windows (which tendency is confirmed by police reports regarding place of entry) and were most likely to enter on the first floor, except in luxury apartment buildings, where entry would probably be less conspicuous at some other floor level. Presumably the first floor was preferred in most instances because it preserved the option of trying the window should the door prove impregnable. Interviewees estimated the entry time required at five minutes for a door and three minutes for a window, and indicated that they would not spend more than a maximum of ten minutes on a door, and five minutes on a window (where they usually felt more exposed).

Interviewees in all categories were also far more likely to simply pry the door or break the window than to use such sophisticated techniques as lock-picking or glass cutting. Consequently, evaluations of interviewees according to the relative "skill" involved in their entry methods resulted in over 80 percent being classed as "semiskilled," as shown below: (See also Appendix Table B(2)-15).

Table 2-7. What Was the Skill Level of the Interviewees,* in Total, and by Age, Race, and Drug Use?

		Age			Race		Drug Use	
	Total	*Under 18*	*18-25*	*Over 25*	*W*	*Non W*	*DU*	*Non DU*
Unskilled	11%	24%	8%	8%	17%	4%	6%	16%
Semiskilled	82	76	86	80	77	89	90	76
Skilled	6	0	6	12	6	7	4	8
Total	97	21	51	25	52	45	48	49

*Skill level was determined by the entry method interviewees predominantly used:

Skilled	— (door)	lockpicking
Semiskilled	— (door)	prying
		attacking lock
		loiding
		passkey
	(window)	prying
		loiding
		cutting glass
Unskilled	— (door)	direct impact
		door open
	(window)	smashing glass
		window open

The predominance of the "semi-skilled" category of burglars was strongly suggested by victimization survey data and police records (see Table 2-8) which indicated that the cruder methods of entry (direct impact, prying door, breaking window glass) are even more common in the real world than in our limited (and admittedly age-biased) sample.

Table 2–8.   Techniques of Portal Entry, Residential Burglary

Door $(N = 219)^a$

Pry door	19.2%
Attack lock	15.0%
Direct Impact	39.3%
Loid door	5.5%
Pick lock	5.0%
Pass key	5.9%
Open door	10.0%
	99.9%

Window $(N = 383)^b$

Break glass	38.0%
Cut glass	1.0%
Pry catch	33.0%
Use open or unlocked window	28.0%
	100.0%

[a]Police reports in the Boston area were largely of the short narrative type and therefore not particularly helpful in pinpointing the specific method of attack used against the door. For example, it was common simply to record "door forced." Therefore, it was necessary to use household survey victimization data for analysis purposes.
[b]Based on Boston Police Records.

Objectives (Appendix B, Tables B(2)-16 and 17)

The particular goods sought and the value of the goods taken reflected both the burglar's perception of his needs and the relative sophistication of his "disposal" methods. Hi-fis, TVs, and radios were sought by almost all the youngest group, who could find a ready market for these items among their own acquaintances. (Police records indicate that electronic equipment is in fact the most common item of loss in reported burglaries.) Older burglars, in contrast, expressed substantially more interest in jewelry and silver, which items generally have greater intrinsic value than TVs, etc., but require more ingenuity to "fence." White burglars were also more likely to seek jewelry and silver than were nonwhites, but otherwise no significant differences appeared associated with race. A fairly consistent interest in cash and lack of interest in credit cards or checks were common to all groups.

The conversion of stolen goods into cash (or cash equivalent, such as drugs) appeared to be accomplished most efficiently by the older group, most of whom disposed of the goods immediately after making a hit. Younger burglars, in comparison, were most likely to take the goods home or to a friend's house, leaving the question of disposal more to chance than to planning. Whites and drug users were also more prompt than their counterparts in divesting themselves of their take.

The same groups most concerned with prompt disposal—the older, white, and drug-using burglars—tended to realize the largest gains from their activities. For example, no drug user and no burglar over 25 admitted to averaging less than $50 per hit, although 35 percent of those under 18 and 18 percent of the nondrug users did so. Similar differences between white and nonwhites were less conspicuous, but nevertheless apparent.

In general the offenders' estimates are slightly below the police reports of actual losses (as noted in Table 2-9), but the reports more nearly reflect actual value of the stolen item while the estimates represent what the offender expects to receive—which is usually 60-80 percent below the actual value of the item.

Table 2–9. Comparison of Actual vs. Estimated Loss

Value of Loss	Police Reports (N = 1673)	Offenders' Estimates
Under $100	21%	23%
$100-$300	38	47
$301-$1000	34	25
Over $1000	7	6

Not surprisingly, the older, white and drug-using groups—those groups which make the largest average scores—tend to perceive their financial needs as correspondingly large. Sixty percent of the older group, for example, asserted that they needed incomes of more than $250/week, compared with only 6 percent of the under-18 group.

Perceived need and average score also partially explain frequency of operation, since (predictably) those who made high average scores tended to operate less frequently and those who needed large amounts of money tended to operate more frequently. This latter observation is particularly applicable to drug users, approximately 80 percent of whom made more than two hits per week. (In contrast, more than 60 percent of the nondrug users made two or less hits per week.)

Motivation

While this study was not equipped to probe offender motivation in great depth, some indications of motivation did emerge in the course of the interview process. Satisfaction of a perceived need for money, of course, appeared the prime motive for most burglaries, although interviewees did acknowledge such subsidiary satisfactions as "excitement, revenge, curiosity" and feelings of group solidarity. Excitement—the challenge of the activity—was mentioned most often by the younger group and least often by the older, who in general appeared less moved by nonprofit considerations than any of the other groups. In spite of these various secondary satisfactions, however, only 10 percent of all the interviewees indicated that they would continue to break and enter if their financial needs were satisfied. Seventy-three percent indicated that "enough money for their needs" (including drugs) would definitely cause an end to their burglarizing and 17 percent were undecided on the question.

Also, although most interviewees came from lower-income backgrounds, their interpretation of their own financial needs had little to do with the basic demands of survival (i.e., food and shelter). As indicated by Appendix B, Table B(2)-18, most of the money obtained from burglary is spent on intoxicants and commercial goods.

These findings can be regarded as lending some support to the theory that relative deprivation—rather than the absolute deprivation behind, say, the theft of a loaf of bread—many account for a large portion of recent increases in criminal behavior. Although real income rose steadily in Boston throughout the 1960s for both whites and nonwhites,[4] the gap between high-income and low-income remains much in evidence. Also, the expectation of low-income groups may have increased out of proportion to actual income increases. Whether this realization of "relative deprivation" is, in fact, responsible for increases in criminal behavior among low-income groups remains a moot question, but some such explanation[5] has also been advanced to account particularly for the disproportionate and apparently increasing[a] number of black offenders, many of whom may have experienced a recent rise in expectations. The present study, however, cannot decide the accuracy of this explanation, since black burglars interviewed for the study did not express motives very different from their white counterparts. If they preferred to attack dwellings owned by whites, they attributed their preference to the belief that whites were simply more affluent.

Finally, much interest in the motivation for criminal behavior has, of late, centered around the relationship between drug use and crime, especially for common crimes such as robbery and burglary. Estimates that addicts account for 50 percent of all property crime have become a common yardstick in discussions of the problem,[6] but the fact that drug use is correlated with criminal behavior does not confirm a causal relationship. Based on a study of addict offenders which showed that most had been delinquent prior to addiction, Kolb[7] suggests that the direction of causality is reversed; namely, that addicts do not become criminals but rather that criminals become addicted to drugs. Support for this argument is also found in a study by Morgan,[8] which indicates that a majority of the adult subjects had criminal records prior to identification as drug users.

---

[a]Between 1965 and 1970, the percentage of nonwhites arrested for burglary rose from 35 to 46 percent, and for robbery, from 56 to 65 percent, while the black population in the city remained constant at about 16 percent.

Kolb[9] also found that heroin use inhibits rather than excites criminal behavior; thus, a burglar who is an addict might be less active than he would be were he not addicted. Similarly, data compiled by the Narcotic Bureau of the Chicago Police Department for 1951[10] indicated that addiction tends to reduce the capacity for careful planning of property crime and the propensity to violent crime. However, Chein and Rosenfeld[11] found that high drug use areas in New York City were ones with increasing property crime; and O'Donnell,[12] in a study of 266 addicts, found that drug use increased the frequency with which individuals engaged in common residential crimes, such as robbery and burglary.

This latter finding was confirmed by the present study. Also, examination of the criminal records of the drug users indicated that drug arrests had preceded burglary charges for two-thirds of the group. However, more than two-thirds had had some criminal arrest before their first drug arrest, which suggests that their involvement in burglary (and drugs) may have been a continuation of their criminal career rather than a result of drug use. It seems clear, however, that drug use accelerated the pace of their burglary activity— and indeed, of all factors analyzed for this study, increase in drug use seems most strongly correlated with recent increases in residential burglary rates in the Boston area. (See page 72.)

Burglar Profiles

Although obviously the age, race, and drug use classifications employed in the preceding discussion overlap extensively, they are sufficiently distinct to permit summary of our observations in the form of brief typological profiles. Interspersed with the following profiles are direct quotations from some of the interviews, which may help convey representative attitudes for each of the types.

The Juvenile Offender. The typical juvenile offender in this study had been arrested a couple of times and placed on probation. Because he lacked both education and experience, he was ill-qualified for legitimate work and demonstrated little skill even in his criminal endeavors. He was more inclined than the older offenders to work with his friends or in gangs, and since he traveled on foot to make his hits, he was more likely to work in or around his own neighborhood, and to rely more on spur-of-the-moment-opportunities than on careful selection of targets. ("I'm just walking down the street and a couple of friends say, 'Hey, do you want to break into a house with us?', I say, 'OK, if its a good hit.' "). He was quite likely to be deterred by evidence of a burglar alarm, police patrols, or unfamiliar neighborhoods, which made him feel conspicuous. His lack of skill led him to prefer easy targets over difficult but affluent ones, and consequently, his average score was low. His disposal of the goods was haphazard rather than systematic, in keeping with his apparent attitude that burglary was more of a game than a way of life.

The 18-25 Year Old Offender.   The extensive overlap between this group and the drug-using group makes the isolation of a distinct age-profile difficult, but a few age-related characteristics may still be noted. The typical burglar in this age range had several previous convictions, but continued to break and enter because he found it easy, not very risky, and relatively lightly punished. ("I gave up mugging because it might end in murder." "I like breaking and entering because you don't have to contend with people.") He was more mobile than the younger burglar and had moved outside his own neighborhood for at least half his hits (over 50 percent—predominantly drug users—did five or more hits a week) and his average score was higher than the juveniles. He also took a wider variety of goods because he had more highly developed channels for disposing of them, and his fences (of whom he had several) were often "so-called respectable citizens."

The Older Offender—Age 25 and Upwards.   The typical older offender had been breaking and entering for many years, and had been in and out of jail several times on many different charges. Like many in the middle age group, he chose breaking and entering as preferable to, and more profitable than, other types of crime. "I purse-snatched when I was 15. I grew out of that into something bigger." "I changed as I learned more . . . from low class neighborhoods to highrise apartments . . . its another step.") That the neighborhood should be affluent was his first consideration and therefore he spent much of his time working in single-family suburban houses. ("When gains don't outbalance the other, you don't take the chance.") He was more inclined to plan carefully, to get to know the neighborhood thoroughly before attempting a hit there, and to employ relatively effective entry methods. ("Any lock made by man can be broken by man.") His average score was higher than that of the other groups and he disposed of the goods immediately through several trusted fences. On the whole, (unless he were a drug addict) he made fewer, more profitable hits, thus reducing the chances of being caught. He was less likely than the younger burglar to be deterred by burglar alarms, which he felt he could "handle," but more likely to be deterred by the presence of an occupant or a dog. Although occasionally he worked at regular employment, he usually had difficulty holding a job, and might have given up trying. ("I don't like to work. I haven't had to work for five years." "You can make a week's pay in one night.")

Whites.   Basically, the methods and skill levels of nonwhite and white burglars were similar, although some relatively minor behavioral differences did emerge from the study. The white burglar was more likely to be married than the black burglar, to have had a semiskilled job, and to have earned a little more money a week. He was more inclined to prefer single-family houses, regardless of the race of the resident, but he was unlikely to work in a predominantly nonwhite residential areas for fear of violence. ("If you get caught in a black or Puerto-Rican neighborhood you might get killed.") The white burglar was also less likely to go into housing projects, more likely to travel further from his home, and more likely to be cautious in hitting the same neighborhood again.

The white burglar gave a higher estimate of the amount of money he needed a week than the black burglar, but since his average score was likely to be a little greater, the frequency of operation was virtually the same for both groups. While approximately the same number in each group were drug users, the white burglar was marginally more likely to be a heroin user.

Blacks. The black burglar generally preferred to hit residences owned by white people, largely because he assumed that they would be more affluent. ("If it was a black guy, I'd know that there wasn't too much money. If it was a white guy, I'd know there was.") However, because he was somewhat less mobile than the white burglar, he was frequently forced to work in relatively less affluent black neighborhoods near his own residence. Many also felt conspicuous and out of place in the suburbs and conceived these areas—along with luxury apartments—to be almost prohibitively well-secured, however attractive as targets. (In response to a slide, "Cops over there all the time. Looks like a white neighborhood. You'd have a police escort every corner you turned.") Blacks, in general, were more likely than whites to be deterred by police patrols, particularly younger blacks.

The black burglar was also more likely to get to his target on foot and to travel less than one hour to make a hit. His average score was marginally lower than the white burglar's, and he was more inclined to take the goods home or to a friend's home than to dispose of them immediately.

The adult black gave a lower estimate of the amount of money he needed a week—between $100 and $250, rather than the $250 or more that the white burglar required. If he was a drug user, he was more inclined to use amphetamines than the white burglar.

The Drug User. The typical drug user in the interviewee sample was under 25, with a drug habit (usually heroin, sometimes amphetamines) of several years standing. He differed from the nondrug user chiefly in that he needed more money and, consequently, made more hits. His habit could cost him $1,500 a week, and rarely cost him less than $150. Since his job, if he still had one, normally earned him between $100 and $200 a week, he had decided to concentrate on breaking and entering because it was the easiest way to get the additional money he needed, and did not involve violence. However, his scores were only a little higher than the nondrug user, and therefore he made many more hits per week—averaging 5-6, compared with 1-2 for the nondrug user. ("On amphetamines you're full of pep, does something to your nervous system. We'd just keep going on and on . . . On one of those benders I might do 150 or 200 burglaries. Before that, I'd only done about 10 a year.")

Although the drug user, in principle, preferred single-family suburban houses where the scores were higher, he was more likely than the nondrug user to work around or in his own neighborhood, particularly as his habit increased. ("When I started doing it, it was always there [single-family suburban houses] . Then I said to heck with going all the way out there. I wanted the junk, right; I'd look for the quickest way to make more money . . .") Because of the urgency with which he needed his money, his view of deterrents was somewhat different from the nondrug user. He did comparatively little planning, and could be more easily deterred by complex security devices. ("If the door was a hassle, I'd go elsewhere.") Although he preferred no one to be home, he was more inclined to be reckless and risk confrontations. ("When I'm strung out . . . I don't care who's at home. I need money.")

The Nondrug User.   Clearly this category includes an analytically intractable cross-section of types, connected only by their common differences with the drug using category. In brief, the nondrug user needed less money, made fewer hits and did more planning. He was more concerned with avoiding personal confrontation and was consequently more likely to be deterred by a full time occupant, by police and security patrols, or even by dogs or neighbors checking on the residence. He was, in contrast, less likely to be deterred by the mechanical obstacles (locks, etc.) which would defeat the patience of the addict. One might also characterize the nondrug user's choice of a career in burglary as more 'disinterested' than the drug user's choice, since (1) the nondrug user was not so obviously incapacitated for legitimate employment and (2) his financial needs were not so extreme as to virtually prohibit living within a legitimate wage.[b]

RESIDENTIAL ROBBERS

Since residential robberies constitute a much smaller percentage of total robberies than do residential burglaries of total burglaries,[c] application of research findings on robbery in general must be made with more caution than was necessary for burglary. Also, residential robbery occurs relatively rarely compared to residential burglary, and, consequently, the accumulation of a workable data base is difficult.

----

[b]Larner and Tefferteller,[13] for example, cite several accounts of addicts who were able to support their habits by legitimate employment until such point as their tolerance for the narcotic increased, i.e., more and more of the drug was required to sustain the same physical and psychological state of well being, at which point it became necessary to supplement and ultimately replace regular jobs with illegal activities.

[c]In Boston, residential robbery annually constitutes less than 10 percent of total robberies, with street robberies comprising the larger percent (66 percent).

The statistics offered in this section, then, must be regarded as quite tentative. No offender interviews were conducted, and only five of the original 39 areas under survey reported a sufficient number of residential robberies to merit any statistical evaluation at all. Nevertheless, the discussion which follows adheres as closely as feasible to the format of the discussion of burglary.

Demographic Characteristics

As is indicated by Table 2-10, robbers—in both Boston and the nation as a whole—are more likely to be nonwhite and slightly older than are residential burglars. Table 2-11, which summarizes the characteristics of offenders involved in the robberies analyzed for this study, indicates a disproportionate representation of black offenders, which is attributable to an inherent bias in the study sample. All of the five areas under study (which were the only areas with significant numbers of residential robberies) were located in the inner city and averaged 55 percent black in population. (See Appendix B, Table B(2)-19.)

Table 2-10. Demographic Characteristics of Persons Arrested for Robbery—1970

	Nationally[a]	US Cities[b]	US Suburbs[c]	Boston[d]
% Male	94%	94%	95%	93%
Median Age	20	19	20	20
% Nonwhite	65	68	40	65

Source: *FBI Uniform Crime Reports 1970*
[a]Tables 28, 30, 32.
[b]Tables 34, 36, 38.
[c]Tables 40, 42, 43.
[d]Source: *Annual Report Police Commissioner for the City of Boston 1970,* Table VIII.

Nevertheless, as Table 2-10 indicates, robbers, like burglars, tend to male, young and black, though perhaps not to the extent indicated in Table 2-11.

Table 2-11. Description of Residential Robbery Offenders—Selected RAs*

Sex (N = 264)	Race (N = 257)	Age (N = 204)
Male — 97%	White — 5%	Under 17 — 12%
Female — 3%	Black — 93%	17 – 20 – 52%
	Other — 2%	21 – 25 – 27%
		Over 25 – 9%

*The numbers were extracted from police records for selected areas. Differences in total numbers reported for each category reflect discrepancies of police reports.

Target Choice

Since residential robbers attack people as well as dwellings, their selection of target is influenced not only by the possibility of gain, risk of detection and ease of access, but also by the added factor of victim resistance. In fact, the access factor as it relates to housing may be relatively inconsequential to the residential robber, who appears more often than not to attack his victim outside the dwelling unit proper. An analysis of residential robberies in the study RAs disclosed that only one-third took place in a dwelling unit, and the remainder in such public areas as hallways and elevators. Of those robberies which did occur inside the dwelling, only 8 percent were in single-family homes and the rest divided between apartment buildings and public housing units. In 90 percent of the cases, the robber entered by the door and in 60 percent, he obtained entry by ruse or threat (i.e., by posing as delivery man or accosting an occupant entering or leaving his home). Of those robberies which occurred outside the dwelling unit but still on residential premises, 65 percent were on the grounds of housing projects, 34 percent in apartment buildings and 1 percent on the property of single-family houses.

Table 2-12 identifies the characteristics of residential robbery victims.

Table 2-12.   Residential Robbery Victim Characteristics

Age (N = 147)	
Under 21	5%
21 - 30	22%
31 - 40	13%
41 - 50	14%
51 - 65	18%
Over 65	28%
Sex (N = 152)	
Male	74%
Female	26%
Race (N = 127)	
White	83%
Black	11%
Other	6%

Based on Police Reports.

The frequent victimization of the over-65 age group may be largely explained by the vulnerability of persons this age to attack. Although Normandeau[14] found greater victimization among younger age groups, his findings applied to robbery of all types, rather than residential robbery in particular. It appears probable that elderly people may be *less* likely than other age groups to be robbed in the course of their business or on the street simply because they are less likely to *be* in business or on the street, but they may be *more* likely to be robbed in or around residences because—in addition to being more vulnerable than other age groups—they spend relatively more time in or close to their homes.[d]

The findings of our research regarding sex and race factors are somewhat more difficult to explain. Females are generally assumed to be more vulnerable than males, and they also outnumber males in the overall city population, yet they account for only about a quarter of the victims of residential robbery. One partial explanation for the disparity in victimization might lie in the fact that our figures do not include figures for larceny pursesnatch, the victims of which are virtually exclusively female. In other words, more men than women may be robbed simply because it is physically more difficult to steal money from a man (who generally carries his wallet close to his person) without some sort of confrontation. When confrontation occurs, the crime is classed as a robbery rather than a larceny.

Also, our figures were taken directly from police records, without being checked by a victimization survey. It is possible, then, that a large number of victimized females did not report the crimes to the police because they were (more than men would be) fearful of violent reprisals.

The last point to be noted is that not all victims of residential robberies are themselves residents of the area in which they are victimized. Indeed, a close analysis of robberies in three of the five surveyed RAs disclosed that one quarter of the victims were nonresidents.

Method of Operation

Planning. According to a Harvard study of robbers in the Boston area, older robbers—like older burglars—tend to be more "professional" than younger ones, to spend more time planning and to be more concerned with locating affluent targets than vulnerable ones.[15]

Predictably, time patterns for robbery tended to differ from those for burglary, since residential robbery requires that people be in or around their homes, and burglary, for the most part, requires the opposite. Consequently, the robberies studied for this project tended to cluster in the late afternoon (when residents would be returning from work or other daily activities) and to some extent, on weekends. As indicated in Table 2-13, no pattern was discernible by month or season.

---

[d]A recent study which found high robbery victimization among the elderly is, Carl L. Cunningham, "Crime and the Aging Victim," *MRI Quarterly* (Kansas City, Mo.) Spring 1973, pp. 4-9.

Table 2–13.   Time Patterns for Residential Robbery

Month (N = 152)					
January	11.8%	May	11.8%	September	5.9%
February	5.9%	June	12.5%	October	8.7%
March	7.2%	July	6.5%	November	9.2%
April	7.2%	August	10.5%	December	3.2%
					99.4%

Day (N = 151)					
Monday	11.2%	Thursday	12.5%	Sunday	11.9%
Tuesday	19.2%	Friday	14.5%		99.6%
Wednesday	10.5%	Saturday	19.8%		

Time (N = 152)	
0:01 A.M. – 6:00 A.M.	12.5%
6:01 A.M. – 12:00 P.M.	15.7%
12:01 P.M. – 6:00 P.M.	42.1%
6:01 P.M. – 12:00 A.M.	29.8%
	100.1%

Methods.   The propensity of robbers to use accomplices—noted in other studies—was confirmed by our survey of residential robberies, 76 percent of which involved two or more perpetrators. The accomplice in robbery apparently serves primarily to increase the threat of force or, if necessary, to aid in applying the force.

The magnitude of the threat used in the cases studied for this project is outlined in Table 2-14.

Table 2–14.   Nature of the Attack

Offender used threat as follows (N = 133)	
Gun	20%
Knife	30%
Blunt object	3%
Physical force	47%
Victims resisted (N = 130)	
Yes	5%
No	95%
Victim injured (N = 99)	
Yes	50%
No	50%
If injured, how (N = 50)	
Shot	0%
Stabbed	12%
Struck by object	8%
Beaten	80%

As indicated above, residential robbery appears relatively dangerous to the victim; although the victim rarely resisted, he was nevertheless injured 50 percent of the time. Similar findings were made by Conklin in his aforementioned study of robbery in the Boston area. Also, as our own findings suggest, and Conklin indicates, the victim of robbery is more likely to be injured by an unarmed assailant than by an armed one.[16] (Note that in Table 2-14, more than 50 percent of the victims were threatened with a weapon, but only 20 percent of those injured were injured with a weapon. One can surmise that most of the remaining 80 percent of the injured were beaten by unarmed assailants.)

Objectives. Naturally enough, robbery of all types primarily involves cash loss, although in the reporting areas under survey, jewelry was taken in 17 percent of the cases and clothing in about 9 percent. The average loss for all residential robbery in Boston in 1970 was $133, whereas the FBI figure for residential robbery nationwide in 1972 was somewhat higher—$262.

NOTES

1. Don C. Gibbons and Donald L. Garrity, "Definitions and Analysis of Certain Criminal Types," *Journal of Criminal Law, Criminology and Police Science* 53 (1962): 28-35.

2. See Marshall B. Clinard and Richard Quinney, *Criminal Behavior Systems, A Typology* (New York: Holt, Rinehart and Winston, 1967): Chapter 7.

3. President's Commission on Law Enforcement and Administration of Justice, *Task Force Report: Crime and Its Impact—An Assessment* (Washington, D.C.: U.S. Government Printing Office, 1967): Chapter 7.

4. A. Ganz and T. Freeman, *Population and Income of the City of Boston* (Boston: BRA, Research Department, 1972): 36.

5. See John Conklin, *Robbery and the Criminal Justice System* (Philadelphia: J.B. Lippincott Co., 1972): p. 36.

6. Op. cit., *Task Force Report: Narcotics,* p. 11, and Max Singer, "The Vitality of Mythical Numbers," *Public Interest* (Spring 1971): 3. An official estimate of the amount of property crime in which addicts are involved in Boston is 40 percent. See Mayor's Committee for the Administration of Justice, *Challenging Crime* (Boston: 1970): 55.

7. Lawrence Kolb, *Drug Addiction: A Medical Problem* (Springfield, Illinois: Charles C. Thomas, 1962).

8. James Morgan, "Drug Addiction: Criminal or a Medical Problem," *Police,* 9 (1965).

9. Op. cit., Kolb.

10. Harold Firestone, "Narcotics and Criminality," *Law and Contemporary Problems* 22 (1957): 69-85.

11. I. Chein and E. Rosenfeld, "Juvenile Narcotic Use," *Law and Contemporary Problems* 22 (1957): 52-68.

12. John A. O'Donnell, "Narcotics Addiction and Crime," *Social*

Problems 13 (1966): 374-384.

13. Jeremy Larner and Ralph Tefferteller, *The Addict in the Street* (New York: Grove Press, Inc., 1964).

14. A. Normandeau, *Trends and Patterns in Crimes of Robbery* (published on demand by University Microfilms Inc., Ann Arbor, Michigan, 1968): Table 61.

15. Op. cit., Conklin: 88-89.

16. Ibid., pp. 112-21.

Chapter Three

Environmental Factors

INTRODUCTION

Observation of the differential distribution of residential crime rates from area
to area prompted an attempt to relate the environmental characteristics of the
various reporting areas to their crime experience. Two basic categories of characteristics were distinguished which might be expected to contribute to the
determination of residential burglary and robbery rates in a given area. The first
category includes social and economic factors which have been frequently cited
in other research as contributing to the formation of a criminal population.
(The assumption here is that areas with, or proximate to, large criminal populations will sustain correspondingly high crime rates—an assumption which appears
justified in view of the relative lack of mobility of the offenders interviewed for
this study.) The second category includes those characteristics of an area
which appear to make the area more or less vulnerable to residential robbers
and burglars. In other words, we hypothesized that high residential crime rates
will correlate with characteristics of neighborhoods which either produce or
attract residential criminals.

Accordingly, the reporting areas (RAs) under study were classified
in terms of relevant social and physical variables and the average annual burglary
rate associated with each classification was then tabulated. (A summary of population characteristics and burglary rates for all study areas—both surveyed and
nonsurveyed—is given in Appendix C, Tables C(2)-1-4.) The following sections
discuss group patterns. Because (as noted in Chapter 2) only five of the RAs
under study reported any significant number of residential robberies, the analysis

focuses on the rates and patterns of residential burglary, with observations on robbery included wherever relevant.

SOCIAL FACTORS

To analyze the relationship between a neighborhood's residential burglary rate and its social characteristics, we selected the following six social indicators for statistical analysis in both a univariate and multivariate framework: geographic location; median income; predominant housing type; racial composition; size of youth population; and burglary rates of surrounding areas. The tabulations of average burglary rates associated with each factor were tested for statistical significance with chi square computations. Findings termed statistically "significant" are so at the .05 level, but other findings which appeared especially suggestive are also presented, even though statistical significance was not achieved.

Geographic Location

While not precisely a "social" factor, geographic location has repeatedly been used as an index to social problems, since the core area of most cities has been found to contain the greatest concentration of social problems and the highest rates of crime.[1] Crime rates have also been found to decrease with distance from the core, and various theories have been advanced to account for this phenomenon. A well known group of criminologists[2] at the University of Chicago, for example, suggested that central city neighborhoods are "zones in transition," adjacent to the thriving city center but characterized by mixed land uses, high industrial concentration, physical deterioration, rented dwellings and transient populations (often foreign-born and nonwhite) who have few ties to the social institutions of the area. The Chicago group argued that rapid turnover of population in such areas was disruptive to institutionalized behavior patterns and therefore conducive to the development of criminal patterns. Although subsequent researchers have differed with the causative aspects of this explanation, the concentration of crime at the city core remains a commonly noted phenomenon in criminological research.

In Boston, the city Core is officially defined by the Statehouse, the historic center of the city, which is adjacent to Park Station, the hub of Boston's subway network. The Core section, which is contained within Police districts 1, 4, 9, and 10 (see Appendix C, Figures C(3)-1-4), includes the downtown business district, a few wealthy residential areas, one university area, and most of the low-income black ghetto. As anticipated above, the average annual residential burglary rate for these areas was significantly higher than that for outlying areas, and rates tended to decrease with distance from the Core, as noted in Table 3-1.

While not statistically significant, the results are suggestive. Most of the core RAs report medium to high rates; and among those which deviate from this pattern, three areas (62, 143, and 602) are luxury high-rise apartment areas

Table 3-1. Average Annual Residential Burglary Rate by Location of Reporting Area (RA)*

Location	Average Annual Rate/1,000 Dwelling Units (DUs)
Core	39
Adjacent to Core	22
Outlying	12

*Not significant at the .05 level.

with special security devices and private guards. RA 600 (a housing project) also reports a low burglary rate, but since (as noted) the area was not surveyed, the reported rate may be incorrect. RA 83's low rate was confirmed by the household survey, but this RA is part of the well-known North End neighborhood, which was cited for its low overall crime rate by Jane Jacobs in the *Death and Life of the Great American Cities* and is discussed in more detail later in this chapter.

Among adjacent RAs there is much more fluctuation in crime rate, ranging from low to high, indicating that factors other than location might have more influence on the residential burglary rate. On the other hand, it is noteworthy that none of the outlying areas have high rates. Also, no outlying areas reported any residential robberies, and four of the five areas reporting significant robbery rates were core areas.

Burglary Rates of Surrounding Neighborhoods

Since the interview data presented in Chapter 2 suggested that burglars do not confine themselves to one type of target (residence, commercial business, etc.) but that many do tend to operate in the same general area, we surmised that the residential burglary for any given area may in part be a function of the overall burglary rate (both residential and nonresidential) of the surrounding neighborhood. A detailed comparison of residential and overall rates is given in Appendix C, Table C(2)-5 and a summary presented in Table 3-2.

Table 3-2. Residential Burglary Rate of RAs by Rate of Surrounding Neighborhood

Surrounding Neighborhood Rate	RA Average Annual Rate/1,000 DUs*
Low	8
Medium	28
High	55

*Statistically significant at the .05 level.

The only exceptions to this tendency within the high rate areas were two with a concentration of well-secured buildings: RA 143, a luxury apartment area with private security arrangements, and RA 166, a housing project which evidenced above average security and maintenance.

Race

The association between the criminal population of a neighborhood and its racial composition has been often noted in criminological literature, although the association appears by no means a simple one. A Baltimore study, for example, found that where blacks constituted less than half the population of an area, the delinquency rate was relatively high, but a substantial concentration of blacks in an area was associated with a low delinquency rate.[3] The same pattern was noted in Washington, D.C., where, in addition, the strong association between the racial heterogeneity of an area and the crime rate was maintained when the income level was controlled for.[4]

The results of the analysis conducted for the present study, however, run counter to the aforementioned patterns, since (as noted in Table 3-3) the average annual rate of predominantly (more than 63 percent black population) black areas was approximately three times that of predominantly white areas (less than 20 percent black population) and approximately one and one-half times that of mixed (20 to 63 percent black) areas.

Table 3–3.   Residential Burglary Rate by Race*

RA Racial Composition	Average Annual Rate/1,000 DUs
White	19
Mixed	40
Black	59

*Statistically significant at the .05 level. See also Appendix C, Table C(2)-6.

Although there was considerable deviation in rates within the white and mixed categories, the only deviation from high rates in predominantly black areas was RA 447, where (as previously noted) the figures may be suspect. However, four of the five areas reporting significant residential robbery rates were mixed, and only one was predominantly black.

Explanations for the association of crime rates with racial composition have frequently centered on the social instability of racially mixed areas,[5] which (it is contended) results in weakened social control over deviant behavior tendencies. Wilkes, for example, concluded that

> The racial composition of an area does have an impact upon the area's crime rate, but we cannot unequivocally assert that certain nationality or racial groups have high rates of crime regardless of

their geographical location, nor can we state that the geographical location exclusively determines the crime rates of such groups. It is necessary to consider the area's ongoing social processes and the social and cultural structure of the relationship between geographical location, racial composition, and area crime rate. In other words, the social integration of the area appears to be of crucial importance in predicting the area's rate of crime and delinquency.[6]

Durkheim also suggested that differential crime rates may be produced by differential degrees of social cohesion and corresponding social control.[7]

However, such explanations would appear inadequate to account for the almost uniformly high crime rates of Boston's predominantly black neighborhoods. Not only do these neighborhoods display a high degree of racial homogeneity,[a] but they also do not appear conspicuously less cohesive than white or mixed neighborhoods. Only 1 of the 4 predominantly black areas included in the household survey for this project ranked 'low' in social cohesion. The other three neighborhoods appeared average in cohesion, along with several white and mixed neighborhoods. While the social cohesion test used in this survey was not intended to provide a definitive evaluation of a neighborhood's social stability, it does suggest that social stability may depend upon a number of, as yet, unmeasurable factors, among which racial composition may be relatively uninfluential. In any case, the covariance of racial composition with other factors such as income and location remains problematical and we will explore it in more detail.

Income

The association of poverty with crime has now become a sociological commonplace, but no single explanation for the association has ever found general acceptance. One fairly influential theory was advanced by a follower of Durkheim, Robert K. Merton, who devised an analytical scheme for predicting the likelihood of criminal and/or deviant behavior on the basis of differential access to the legitimate means of achieving success goals.[8] Also basing his work on the notion that lower class persons are frustrated in their efforts to achieve success, Cohen[9] argued that lower class boys "stand the values on their heads" by developing behaviors antithetical to conventional middle class values.

More recently, Cloward and Ohlin[10] have developed a theory of delinquency causation, also based on the seminal contributions of Durkheim and Merton, which takes account not only of the distribution of access to legitimate channels, but also of the differential availability of illegitimate alternatives. Cloward and Ohlin posit the existence of three distinct types of

---

[a]Although "63 percent or more black population" defined areas to be considered "black" in Table 3-3, in reality Boston's black neighborhoods average around 85 percent black, with few as low as 60 percent, and several as high as 95 or 96 percent.

delinquent subculture—conflict, retreatist, and criminal—based on differential access to legitimate and illegitimate opportunities. By implication from their analysis, property crimes such as burglary, would most likely occur in contexts where avenues to legitimate success are closed to upcoming youth, but where three is an established criminal network (e.g., "fences") through which success strivings may be channeled. In a similar analysis, Spergel[11] suggested that a theft subculture grows out of a social contradiction in which there are partially limited conventional and criminal opportunities by which to achieve success goals.

In contrast to theories which relate crime to social disorganization or paucity of social and economic resources, some writers have suggested that crime is to some extent an unintended consequence of affluence: increases in crime, it is argued, may stem from increased prosperity and leisure, in that there are more and more goods to steal and more and more time in which to do it.[12]

Detailed analysis of the effects of income level on criminal behavior was outside the scope of the present project. However, the association between low income levels and high crime rates was confirmed and is indicated in Table 3-4:

Table 3–4.   Residential Burglary Rate by Income

RA Income Level[a]	*Average Annual Rate/1,000 DUs*[b]
Lower (below $5,000)	47
Middle ($5,000-$8,000)	27
Higher (above $8,000)	13

[a]This definition of income provides for a relative ranking of an area rather than an absolute one, since the areas under study are predominantly lower and lower-middle income on an absolute scale.
[b]Statistically significant at the .05 level. See also Appendix C, Table C(2)-7.

As is apparent from the table, the average annual rate of the lower income neighborhoods was more than 1½ times that of the middle income neighborhoods and more than 3½ times that of the upper income neighborhoods. Also, all five of the areas reporting significant robbery rates were low income areas. However, a number of areas deviate from the pattern at all income levels, and predominantly black areas deviate with particular consistency. As indicated in Tables 3-5 and 3-6, burglary rates increase with income in black areas and decrease with income in white areas (although there is a slight tendency for rates to rise in high income areas).

Also, our regression analysis indicated that burglary rates tend to rise with income in suburban areas, although no suburban area evidenced a high rate.

The variation of burglary rates among neighborhoods of comparable income level suggests that, while high average crime rates appear generally

Table 3–5. Residential Burglary Rate by Income in Black RAs

RA Income Level[a]	RAs	Average Annual Rate/1,000 DUs[c]
Lower income[b]	(256, 265, 296, 297, 589)	54
Middle income[b]	(306, 307, 308, 315, 319, 447)	62

[a]There were no higher income black areas.
[b]If RA 447 is eliminated, the rate is 69.
[c]Differences between group rates not significant at .05 level.

Table 3–6. Residential Burglary Rate by Income in White RAs

RA Income Level	RAs	Average Annual Rate/1,000 DUs[b]
Lower income[a]	(622, 135, 196)	53
Middle income	(57, 62, 70, 83, 214, 602, 775, 779, 824)	10
Higher income	(134, 143, 232, 421, 505, 530, 653, 720, 736, 745)	12

[a]If RA 196 is eliminated, the rate is 74.
[b]Differences in group rates significant at .05 level.

associated with low average income areas, income alone will not determine an area's rate. In addition, while income appears to operate as a factor in the development of a criminal population (i.e., low income areas frequently breed large criminal populations and consequently sustain high crime rates), it also appears to operate with the reverse effect as a factor in the criminal decision-making process. That is, while burglars are more likely to be found in lower income neighborhoods, within any given neighborhood they are likely to select the more affluent targets. Thus, for example, suburban neighborhoods in general have lower average burglary rates than do the lower-income city neighborhoods, but victimization within the suburban neighborhoods tends to fall on the more affluent areas.

Age

The relationship between the factor of age and the commission of crimes against property was anticipated in Chapter 2, which reported the median age of 18 for arrested burglars and 20 for robbers. This relationship has also been documented in other criminological literature, much of which has been devoted to the problem of juvenile delinquency. A study conducted by the Gluecks,[13] for example, found that 76 percent of a sample of juvenile delinquents committed crimes against property; 5 years later, 74 percent; 10 years later, 51 percent; and 15 years later, 42 percent. The decline in commission of property offenses, however, was offset by an increase in sex offenses and drunkenness. Other studies have noted a similar effect of aging—"burning out"—which results in the termination of a career in property crime at the onset of middle age or sooner.

Accordingly, we hypothesized that areas with large populations under the age of 18 would have correspondingly large criminal populations and consequently sustain high burglary rates, which hypothesis proved to be at least partially valid, as indicated in Table 3-7.

Table 3-7. Residential Burglary Rate by Under 18 Population

Under 18 Population in RA	Average Annual Rate/1,000 DUs*
Less than 20%	37
Less than 30% . . .	18
Less than 40%	19
Over 40%	41

*Difference between groups not significant at .05 level. See also Appendix C, Table C(2)-8.

The clearest pattern is found at the over 40 percent level. If RAs 196 and 447, where the figures are suspect, were eliminated from the over 40 percent group, the rate increases to 51 and all remaining areas have at least a medium rate. Most of the areas are housing projects, located in or near the core area with large black low income populations. Although clearly all these factors interact in such areas, projects, nevertheless, tend to be victimized primarily by young persons who live in the vicinity. For example, an analysis of all arrests for burglary in RA 256 (a large housing project) during the years 1970 and 1971 disclosed that out of a total of 78 persons arrested, 30 percent were under 17, and the rest were all between 17-24. Eighty-one percent of all persons arrested lived in the project.

The lack of any apparent relationship between burglary rates and size of youth population in areas of relatively low yough population, suggests that these areas may not be victimized by residents but may offer particular attractions as targets for nonresidents. In fact, the three areas in this group displaying the highest burglary rates (RAs 135, 145, and 622) are all located in core areas of mixed commercial-residential land use, with large transient populations residing for the most part in relatively old and large, multiunit buildings. All three of the areas are also low income, although at least two of the three appear to contain large student populations, which may be technically "low income" but in fact display fairly affluent life styles. All of these factors—the transient population, relatively unsecured buildings, affluent life styles, and convenient location—may act as attractions to offenders in surrounding neighborhoods.

Predominant Housing Type

The relationship between the spatial configuration of a residence and its crime experience has received particular attention of late as a result of Newman's concept of defensible space.[14] Newman found that impersonal high-rise buildings generally evidenced much higher crime rates than did the more 'human-scale' low-rise buildings, and to correct this situation, he advocated specific changes in physical design aimed at increasing the territorial concern of residents. He pointed out, for example, that corridors, stairways, and grounds which are related to specific dwelling units (through landscaping, partitioning, and positioning) are more likely to be maintained and observed by residents than are large anonymous spaces.

The present study lacked the resources to evaluate the particular design recommendations put forth by Newman and other researchers, but an attempt was made to test the hypothesis that large, impersonal buildings provide atmospheres conducive to crime. RAs were classified according to their predominant housing type in the following manner:[b]

1. Single-family structures;
2. Small multifamily structures, 2-9 units (usually walk-up);
3. Large multifamily structures, 10 or more units (often elevator buildings);
4. Public housing projects (While not a type of housing in the physical sense, it was felt that the public housing areas were sufficiently unique to require a separate analysis.)

The crime rate of each housing type is shown in Table 3-8.

Table 3-8. Residential Burglary Rate by RAs Predominant Housing

Housing Type	Average Annual Rate/1,000 DUs*
Single-family	14
Small Multiunit	30
Public Housing	34
Large Multiunit	37

*Differences between group rates not statistically significant at the .05 level. See also Appendix C, Table C(2)-9.

---

[b]In most areas predominant type was determined according to which type had the largest percentage of units in the total housing stock. The exceptions were 505, where there were slightly more small multiunit dwellings than single-family, and 70, 145, 307, and 622, where SMUs prevailed over large multiunits. For those areas the rating was based on site observers' judgments of which type best characterized the RA and on the type of housing sustaining burglaries.

The fact that areas where single-family housing predominates have a markedly lower rate than the others may be less a result of structure than other covariant factors such as location in outlying areas.

If RAs 196 and 600, where figures are suspect, are removed from the housing project group, its rate increases to 43/1,000. Also, 4 of the 5 areas with significant robbery rates were housing projects.

If the luxury high-rise areas are removed from the large multiunit sample, the average rate rises to 57/1,000 units. This suggests the possibility that large structures may be positively correlated with burglary. Only RA 421 deviated from this pattern, and its crime rate was not tested by the household survey. However, in Chapter 4 an analysis of victimization fails to support a significant relationship between burglary rates and housing type.

Statistical Evaluation of Social Factors

The social factors and area burglary rates discussed in the preceding sections were analyzed with univariate regression equations, which confirmed the correlation between burglary rates and both the percent nonwhite population and the surrounding neighborhood rates. (See Appendix C, Tables C(2)-10 and 11.) Regression results for median income showed significantly decreasing burglary rates with increasing income, except in suburban areas and in predominantly black areas wherein both the relationship between rates and income is reversed. (See Appendix C, Tables C(2)-12 and 13.) Since these two areas occupy the extremes of the rate spectrum (suburban areas with consistently lower rates and black areas with consistently higher rates) it appears probable that, for these extremes, income assumes importance as a factor in target selection, in addition to its role as a social factor associated with the number of burglars in the local population. (That is, while a low income level appears to correlate in general with a large neighborhood burglar population, many burglars prefer the more affluent neighborhoods.) The pattern of increasing rates with increasing youth population was also confirmed by regression analysis after the areas of low youth population (less than 20 percent under 18) were removed from the sample. Again, no correspondence between rates and number of youth could be observed for these areas. (See Appendix, Table C(2)-14.)

Finally, efforts to test the supposition that large impersonal structures create an atmosphere conducive to crime were impeded by the lack of a meaningful housing variable. The one used in our regression analysis—the proportion of dwelling units in buildings of more than 10 units—was too general to reveal any real correlation between housing types and burglary rates. Clearly the wide diversity of populations, security practices, and income levels among high-rise luxury apartment buildings and high-rise housing projects makes size alone a meaningless measurement, but no more refined criteria could be established within the time-frame of our study. (See Appendix C, Table C(2)-15.)

The central problem in the investigation of the influences of all these variables obviously lies in their tendency to covary in the real world. The statistical association between the crime rate and the racial composition of the neighborhood, for example, may only reflect negative correlation between income and percent nonwhite, with income being the causal variable in the determination of residential crime rates.

This extensive collinearity between the independent or explanatory variables can be seen clearly from the following correlation matrix.

Table 3-9. Correlation Matrix of Regression Variables

	Income	Race	Youth	Structure	Surrounding Neighborhood Rate
Income	1.0	−.36	−.11	−.27	−.24
Race	−.36	1.0	.56	−.06	.50
Youth	−.11	.56	1.0	.09	−.08
Structure	−.27	−.06	.09	1.0	.35
Neighborhood rate	−.24	.50	−.08	.35	1.0

Thus, the income variable is seen to be negatively correlated with all four additional variables; high positive correlation also exists between race and age composition of the neighborhood.

In an effort to disentangle the effects of the variables, we applied the multivariate equation presented in the following table to a sample of areas which excluded those of either particularly high income or particularly low youth populations. (These areas were removed from the sample because, as noted previously, their burglary rates appear to vary independently of the social factors under present consideration.)

Table 3-10. Multivariate Regression Results; Major Subsample*

$$Y = a_0 + \sum_{K=1}^{5} a_K X_K$$

Y = Reported residential burglary rate per 1,000 occupied dwelling units.

X_1 = Median income of RA in hundreds.

X_2 = Mean number of household members below 18 years of age in RA.

X_3 = % of nonwhite residents in RA.

X_4 = % of RA dwelling units in buildings of over 10 units.

X_5 = Average total burglary rate of the neighborhood in which the RA is situated per 1,000 population.

Table 3-10. Continued

a_0	a_1	a_2	a_3	a_4	a_5	$\bar{R}^2$	F
61.6	−.428					.10	2.92
(3.75) + (−1.71)							
4.68		25.8				.16	4.83
(0.32)		(2.20)					
10.8			.554			.56	32.3
(1.88)			(5.68)				
30.5				.206		.04	1.04
(4.21)				(1.02)			
−1.53					.195	.49	23.90
(−0.18)					(4.89)		
−42.7	.463	9.78	.442	.135	.081	.63	7.07
(−1.47)	(.163)	(0.77)	(1.76)	(.609)	(0.91)		

*Note: Numbers in parentheses are t values.

The results presented in this table show race to be the most significant predictor of burglary rates, followed by the rates of the surrounding areas. However, the covariance of race with income and size of youth population has already been noted, and burglary rates of surrounding neighborhoods are just as likely to represent socioeconomic continuity as to represent a causative factor of crime patterns.

VULNERABILITY FACTORS

In contrast to those theories which focus on the development of criminal populations and aim ultimately at a reduction of the number of criminals, a body of criminological research has concentrated on the reduction of crime through the foreclosure of criminal opportunities[c]—the assumption being that it is easier to alter the environment which provides such opportunities than to alter the complex social and economic forces which contribute to criminal motivation. The remaining sections of this chapter discuss five "opportunity" factors commonly cited in criminological literature as determinants of an area's vulnerability to crime. The factors are: level of access or physical vulnerability of structures and areas (urban design factors, portal security systems), social cohesion of areas, occupancy patterns, visibility of targets, and deployment of police or other patrol forces. Since three of these factors—(access, visibility and occupancy)—are also characteristics of individual structures as well as of

[c]Opportunity reduction also subsumes measures which increase risk.

whole areas, they are discussed again and in more detail in Chapter 4, which deals with variations in victimization of individual persons and buildings *within* areas of comparable victimization rates. For the moment, however, we are primarily concerned with identifying broad patterns of victimization from area to area, so the discussion which follows is necessarily generalized and somewhat impressionistic.

Access or Physical Vulnerability

Some relatively recent writers—most prominent among them, Newman and Jacobs—have examined the influence of an area's physical design—its accessibility, land use characteristics, location in relation to parks, parking lots, etc.—upon its crime rate. Jacobs, for example, argued that specialized activity areas (residential, commercial, industrial, etc.) tended to segment the city, eliminate citizen surveillance of streets, and thereby improve opportunities for crime. Her solution, formed after the model of Greenwich Village and Boston's North End, was to encourage diverse land use (mixed purpose neighborhoods) which would promote maximum street activity at all times and thus enhance possibilities for voluntary surveillance.[15] Similarly, Luedtke, Angel, and Newman[16] agreed that the undertrafficked interior grounds of housing projects are hazardous because they lack the informal surveillance of regular users. However, whereas Angel urges that pedestrians be encouraged to traverse the grounds, Newman maintains that overly accessible grounds will attract criminal elements and that pedestrians should, therefore, be routed around border streets.

While the present study was not intended to evaluate such urban design issues in detail, the apparent contradiction noted above also surfaced in the on-site surveys conducted for the study. That is, while some areas of mixed land use and heavy street use (notably the North End) did in fact evidence low robbery and burglary rates, other mixed areas (notably, RA 145—Prudential-Copley Square neighborhood—and RA 622—Kenmore Square neighborhood) evidenced the highest rates of any of the surveyed areas. The neighborhoods surrounding RA 145 and RA 622 both contain a mixture of cultural and academic centers, offices, stores, bars, and residential buildings, ranging from high-income apartments to deteriorated multifamily dwellings. The three areas (RAs 83, 145, and 622) may differ in other aspects of physical layout, but these differences appeared relatively minor compared to the differences in population composition. RA 83, the North End, is occupied primarily by low-middle income Italians, most of whom have long-term family ties to the North End and who share a common religion, language, and cultural tradition. The other two areas are occupied primarily by mixed transient populations—RA 145, by low-middle income working people, many of whom are single, and RA 622, by young white transients, many of whom are students.

In addition to general observations of the land use composition of areas, the site surveys included day and night observations of traffic conditions, which were defined as follows:

1. *Light traffic*—generally very few or no passing vehicles over a period of 10-15 minutes.
2. *Moderate traffic*—generally a steady flow of passing vehicles every few minutes.
3. *Heavy traffic*—generally a continuous flow of passing vehicles.

Pedestrian traffic was also classified as light, moderate, and heavy, and notice was taken of residents in yards and in streets in order to estimate outdoor activity in the neighborhood.

No clear pattern emerged from the analysis of traffic patterns. Again, both RAs 83 and 622 had many people on the street late at night, yet the former had low and the latter high victimization. RA 505 had few people on the street and a low victimization rate.

In fact, the only areas in which physical "access" characteristics appeared consistently correlated to burglary and robbery rates were in the luxury high rise apartment areas (RAs 143, 602, and 62), all of which displayed elaborate security precautions, low burglary rates, and no robberies. Typical of this group, RA 62, for example, is located in downtown Boston and is comprised of the Charles River Park Apartments, which include four high-rise apartment complexes, a few single-family town houses, a restaurant and various recreational facilities for residents, most of whom have middle to high incomes. Security guards are on duty day and night at entrances to the complex, and entrances to the individual buildings can be seen either directly by guards or via closed-circuit TV cameras, which operate 24 hours a day.

While these areas appeared the only ones in which conspicuous physical similarities were related to conspicuous similarities in crime experience, two additional considerations must be kept in mind. First, "high-rise" is a type of structure, not a characteristic of areas, although in this survey enough such structures clustered to form distinct areas. Second, "luxury high-rise" by definition denotes the residence of a particular class of people (middle to upper income, usually with few children). The very low victimization rate would probably not hold for an area containing few rather than a concentration of such structures. Also, the same level of security would be difficult to impose with a different population group (e.g., low income families with many children).

Finally, in addition to evaluating overall area-access characteristics, the household survey also analyzed the security of dwelling portals (doors and windows) in reference to federal standards; but since so few portals met the standard, areas could not be ranked according to portal security of their component dwellings. Consequently, the information obtained from the analysis is included in Chapter 4, which deals with the victimization of individual structures.

Social Cohesion

The influence of social cohesion on the crime experience of an area has already been mentioned in conjunction with the factors which may contribute to the formation of a criminal population (see Chapter 3). However, social cohesion has also been cited as a factor in crime detection and deterrence, since (it is argued) socially cohesive areas are most likely to evidence the informal but effective surveillance systems which identify and discourage criminal strangers. In fact, much of the current interest in physical design as a crime control strategy can be traced to the belief (again, enunciated by Jacobs and Newman, among others) that proper design can foster territorial concern and thereby reduce opportunities for crime. The influence of social cohesion was also suggested by the preceding discussion of physical access characteristics, which noted that Boston's low crime North End appeared to differ more drastically from high crime areas in its social composition than in its physical layout.

In order to obtain some rough measurement of the quality of social cohesion, the household survey phase of the present project developed an index of social cohesion based upon the answers to the following three questions:

1. In some neighborhoods people do things together and help each other—in other neighborhoods people mostly go their own ways. In general, what kind of neighborhood would you say this is mostly—one where people *help each other* or one where people *go their own ways*?

   ☐ *Help each other*

   ☐ *Go their own ways*

2. How many families around here do you feel you know well enough to ask a favor, of if you needed something—would you say *most* of them, *some* of them or *almost none* of them?

   ☐ *Most*

   ☐ *Some*

   ☐ *Almost none*

3. And how long have you been living at this address?

The areas were rated low, medium, or high in degree of social cohesion, based on the following scale. One point (each) was given if a person knew almost none of his neighbors, had lived at his present address less than two years, or said that people in the neighborhood went their own way. Two points (each) were given if a person knew some of his neighbors, or had lived at his present address two to five years. Three were given if a person knew most of his neighbors, said they help each other, or had lived there more than five years. Those who received an average score that was less than 1.6 were defined as "low," between 1.6 and 2.5 were defined as "medium," and those with 2.6 or more were defined as "high." Any RA where 40 percent or more responses fell into the low category was defined as "low"; RAs where 40 percent or more fell into the "high" category were defined as "high" in cohesion.

As Table 3-11 indicates, the burglary rate was inversely related, although not significantly, to this social cohesion measure.

Table 3-11.   Residential Burglary Rate by Degree of Social Cohesion

Degree of Social Cohesion[a]	*Average Annual Rate/1000 DUs*[b]
Low	90
Medium	28
High	16

[a]Includes only RAs included in household survey.
[b]Differences between groups not significant at the .05 level. See also Appendix C, Table C(2)-16.

Not surprisingly, the North End neighborhood ranked highest in social cohesion, and lowest in need of police service (as measured by percentage of residents who call police annually, see Appendix C, Table C(2)-17). Other highly cohesive areas (RAs 57 and 505) also displayed low burglary rates, as did the nonsurveyed but similar white ethnic areas (RAs 214, 232, 824).

Occupancy

Since, as noted in Chapter 2, the overwhelming majority of burglaries are directed against unoccupied premises, and since the effectiveness of the kind of neighborhood surveillance system discussed in the preceding section will depend in part on the amount of time people spend in or around their neighborhoods, it seemed probable that the burglary rate of an area would reflect occupancy patterns of the residents. As a test of this hypothesis, the surveyed RAs were tanked as follows:

1. *High Occupancy:* RAs where 60 percent or more of the dwellings were unoccupied in the daytime no more than five hours a week.
2. *Low Occupancy:* RAs where 60 percent of the dwellings were unoccupied in the daytime more than 35 hours a week.
3. *Medium Occupancy:* RAs where dwellings did not fall into either of the above categories.

The results are contained in Table 3-12.

As the table indicates, the low occupancy areas were frequently victimized; medium and high occupancy areas showed a much lower victimization rate on the average, but the rates for individual areas within these categories

Table 3-12. Average Annual Residential Burglary Rate by Dwelling Occupancy

RA Occupancy Level[a]	Average Annual Rate/1000 DUs[b]
Low occupancy	94
Medium occupancy	27
High occupancy	28

[a]Includes only RAs in household survey.

[b]Differences between groups not significant at the .05 level. See also Appendix C, Table C(2)-18.

varied greatly. The relationship between low occupancy and victimization of individual dwellings within RAs is discussed in Chapter 4.

Visibility

Although it is commonly assumed that lighting constitutes a major deterrent to crime, few studies document this assumption in any detail. Several articles have reported major reductions in crime after the installation of improved lighting systems,[17] but the crimes referred to are generally nonresidential—e.g., street robbery, school vandalism, commercial burglary.

One Detroit study did inspect the site of residential burglaries and rated street lighting "inadequate from a crime reduction standpoint" in 50 percent of the blocks surveyed and 88.2 percent of the alleys. Only 11.1 percent of the burglarized structures were found to have "adequate" side or rear lighting, although entry from these directions accounted for 77 percent of all burglaries in the city.[18] Although the study hypothesized a correlation between lighting and residential crime, apparently no systematic attempt was made to determine whether lighting in the surveyed premises was significantly poorer than in nonvictimized locations.

Some of the difficulties in assessing the impact of lighting on residential crimes undoubtedly arise from the fact that residential crimes are, by definition, low-visibility crimes; they take place off the street and generally out of view of police or passers-by. Also, the most common residential crime, burglary, most often occurs in the daytime, which renders the lighting issue irrelevant.

In general, the municipal lighting in the areas surveyed for this study was much the same from area to area, but even where differences were noted, no correlation could be established with robbery and burglary rates. RA 70 (Beacon Hill), for example, appeared the most poorly lit,[d] yet this area experienced few nighttime burglaries, many daytime burglaries, and no residential robberies.

[d]By choice of residents, who prefer the quaint "gas-style" lamps found in this area to the more efficient standard-lumen municipal fixtures.

Overall, the influence on visibility of such physical characteristics as landscaping, alleys, parking lots, etc. appeared more critical in relation to residential crime than did the influence of lighting *per se.* Although the relationship between these physical characteristics and burglary rates varied considerably among the RAs, most of the RAs (e.g., 50, 265, 291, and 736) with many dwelling portals made unobservable by vacant lots, alley ways, shrubs or other obstructions displayed medium to high burglary rates and most of the RAs where portals could be easily seen (e.g., RA 505, 57, and 134) displayed low rates. The only dramatic exception to this observation was, again, the North End, which had a low rate but also low visibility of entrances, many of which were located off side alleys or small back streets. However, as previously noted, the North End appears something of an anomaly in criminological literature.

Police Protection

Although police are commonly thought of as the first line of defense against crime, their actual effectiveness against residential crimes seems extremely doubtful. Of approximately 2,000 police reports on burglaries analyzed for this study, less than one percent of the crimes were discovered in progress by patrolling police. An additional six percent were discovered while still in progress by citizens who summoned the police, and the remaining 93 percent of the crimes were not discovered until sometime after they were committed. Only four percent of the cases surveyed resulted in arrests, of which approximately half took place at the scene of the crime, and the other half, through detective follow-up investigation. As indicated in Table 3-13, arrest findings for the present study are similar to those of a study of police apprehension activities undertaken in New York City:

Table 3–13. Comparative Arrest Index for Burglary

City	Cases	Arrest Index	Detective Arrest Index
Boston (39 RAs)	1,860	.04	.02
New York*	67,028	.04	.01

*Peter W. Greenwood, *An Analysis of the Apprehension Activities of the New York City Police Department* (New York: Rand Institute, 1970), p. 6.

These rather bleak findings are not surprising in view of the low visibility of burglary and the fact that most of these crimes occur in unoccupied dwellings.

Residential robbery raises similar problems, although the police seem to have somewhat more success in ultimately making arrests. One study of robbery[19] in the Boston area found that of a total of 69 residential robberies occuring in the first six months of 1968, none were actually observed by patrolling police, but 46 percent were eventually cleared by arrest. However, only 15 percent of these arrests were made at the scene of the crime, which amounted to fewer on-scene arrests for residential robbery than for any other type of robbery. Only 23 percent of the residential robbery arrests surveyed for the present study took place on the scene, but again, the number of cases was too small to permit any conclusions.

As regards the overall amount of police protection available to Boston area residents, Table 3-14 indicates that Boston area police departments have more personnel per capita than do police departments in other areas of the country.

Table 3-14. Comparative Ratio of Police to Population—1970

City	Sworn Personnel/ 1000 Population	National Average for Cities of a Similar Size*
Boston	4.36	2.8
Newton	2.28	1.5
Norwood	1.5	1.5

*FBI *UCR 1970,* Table 51.

However, the relative amount and effectiveness of protection against residential crime in each of the surveyed RAs could not be assessed because (1) police deployment is normally based on overall workload, of which residential crime is only a small part, and (2) a police patrol beat in Boston generally encompasses several RAs, which makes any calculation of patrol units vs. burglary and robbery rates meaningless.

The household survey phase of the present project did make some attempt to assess relative police protection through consumer evaluations, but since—with only one exception[e]—all-white RAs gave favorable ratings and mixed or black areas gave unfavorable ratings, no conclusions could be reached as to whether the ratings reflected reality or merely racial and class attitudes. Also, none of the areas had instituted citizen patrols, so this protective measure could not be evaluated. Chapter 5 contains a more detailed discussion of the role, and potential role, of police in controlling residential crimes.

CONCLUSIONS

The foregoing analysis of the distribution of residential burglary rates emphasizes the relationship between income, geographic location, and vulnerability. Since ample research has identified the inner city areas as those where crime and other social problems are concentrated, "location" can be taken to represent

[e]The one exception was a white housing project area, which gave police protection a low rating.

the coalescence of social and economic factors discussed earlier. We may then summarize the most critical factors in the differential distribution of residential burglary rates among areas as: the location of the neighborhood; the affluence of the residents; and the vulnerability of the dwelling (measured by its physical accessibility and protection, occupancy, visibility, and the social cohesion of the neighborhood).

The relative weight of these factors in accounting for victimization rates, however, appears to differ substantially from one area to another. An analysis of discernible patterns illustrates this contention.[f]

In areas where either social cohesion was high or there was a concentration of access-secure buildings (RAs, 83, 57, 505, 143, 602, and 62) the burglary rate was low, regardless of location or affluence. In these areas, dwelling units were made relatively invulnerable, either by protective measures or by the presence of concerned and watchful neighbors.

Among less obviously secure or cohesive areas, burglary rates appeared most influenced by geographic location, with rates generally inversely proportional to distance from the metropolitan core. However, the precise interplay of forces within the inner (core and adjacent) and outer zones differed according to particular characteristics of the area. For outlying areas (all of which had low or medium burglary rates and none of which had highly cohesive populations or concentrations of well-secured dwellings), affluence appeared the key determinant in differentiating the rates from neighborhood to neighborhood. The relatively higher rates of the more affluent suburban neighborhoods (RAs 736 and 745) were anticipated by the information obtained from the burglar interviews, which indicated that these neighborhoods tend to be victimized to a greater extent by more skilled burglars who value affluent targets more highly than vulnerable ones.

In inner city areas with relatively high crime rates, however, the interplay of environmental factors becomes more complex. For example, one large public housing project (RA 256) with a predominantly low income non-white population had a high incidence of residential burglary, despite better than average police patrol and portal security. Since most offenses were committed by youths who resided in the project, the high crime rate is probably a function of social characteristics which produce offenders.

Another area (RA 622) comprised predominantly of multiunit apartments occupied by young, unmarried white persons showed a similarly high burglary rate, which in this case could be explained by vulnerability factors: a low level of social cohesion and also a low dwelling occupancy rate during the day. Still other areas (RA 315), not differing greatly from the average in vulnerability characteristics, income, or social problems, showed unexpectedly high burglary

---

[f]Characteristics of the RAs discussed in the following analysis are briefly summarized in Appendix C with the exception of RAs 143, 602 and 62, which are luxury high-rise areas not included in the household survey.

rates—probably just as a result of their proximity to less affluent, high crime areas.

While the presence of or proximity to a large low-income youth population may account for the high crime rates of some housing projects and adjacent areas, vulnerability appears to be the most generally influential factor in differentiating crime rates of neighborhoods within the inner city area. The burglars who work in the inner city tend to value ease of access more highly than the likelihood of substantial gain. Consequently, conspicuously vulnerable areas in the inner city tend to display high burglary rates more consistently than do conspicuously affluent areas.

The foregoing suggests that the probability of an area's residential burglary victimization follows in ascending order:

1. Areas with a highly cohesive population or a concentration of access-secure buildings regardless of location.
2. Outlying, nonaffluent areas.
3. Outlying affluent areas.
4. Inner areas that are not highly vulnerable.
5. Inner areas that are highly vulnerable.

NOTES

1. Judith A. Wilkes, "Ecological Correlates of Crime and Delinquency," *Task Force Report: Crime and Its Impact—An Assessment* (Washington, D.C.: U.S. Government Printing Office, 1967): 146. See also: Calvin S. Schmid, "Urban Crime Areas: Part I," *American Sociological Review* 25 (August 1960): 527-542, and "Urban Crime Areas: Part II," *American Sociological Review* 25 (October 1960): 655-678. Sarah L. Boggs, "The Ecology of Crime Occurrence in St. Louis: A Reconceptualization of Crime Patterns," A Dissertation, Washington University, 1964. Richard Quinney, "Crime, Delinquency, and Social Areas," *Journal of Research in Crime and Delinquency* 1 (1964): 149-154. Stanley Turner, "The Ecology of Delinquency" in *Delinquency: Selected Studies,* T. Sellin, and M. Wolfgang, eds. (New York: John Wiley and Sons, Inc., 1969). Robert Gold, "Urban Violence and Contemporary Defensive Cities," *Journal of the American Institute of Planners* 36 (May 1970): 154.

2. See Frederick M. Thrasher, *The Gang* (Chicago: University of Chicago Press, 1927): Clifford R. Shaw and Henry E. McKay, *Juvenile Delinquency and Urban Areas* (Chicago: University of Chicago Press, 1942).

3. Bernard Lander, *Toward an Understanding of Juvenile Delinquency* (New York: Columbia University Press, 1954).

4. V.V. Willie and A. Gershenovitz, "Juvenile Delinquency in Racially Mixed Areas," *Americal Sociological Review* 29 (October 1964): 740-744.

5. Ibid.

6. Op. cit., Wilkes, p. 146. See also Robert Angell, "The Social

Integration of American Cities of More Than 100,000 Population," *American Sociological Review* 12 (June 1947): 335-342.

7. Emile Durkheim, *Rules of Sociological Method,* 8th ed. trans: Sarah A. Solvag and John H. Mueller, ed. George E.G. Catlin (New York: The Free Press, 1951).

8. Robert K. Merton, "Social Structure and Anomie," *American Sociological Review* 3 (October 1938): 672-682. For a revised and expanded version of Merton's article, see Robert K. Merton, *Social Theory and Social Structure* (New York: The Free Press, 1957).

9. Albert K. Cohen, *Delinquent Boys* (New York: The Free Press, 1955).

10. Richard A. Cloward and Lloyd E. Ohlin, *Delinquency and Opportunity* (New York: The Free Press, 1960).

11. Irving Spergel, *Racketville, Slumtown, Haulberg* (Chicago: University of Chicago Press, 1964).

12. See Lloyd E. Ohlin, "The Effect of Social Change on Crime and Law Enforcement," *Notre Dame Lawyer* 43 (1968): 834-846.

13. Sheldon Glueck and Eleanor Glueck, *Juvenile Delinquents Grow-Up* (Cambridge: Harvard University Press, 1940).

14. Oscar Newman, *Defensible Space* (New York: The MacMillan Company, 1972).

15. Jane Jacobs, *The Death and Life of Great American Cities* (New York: Random House, 1961).

16. Gerald Luedtke and Associates, *Crime and the Physical City,* (Detroit: by the Author, 1970), Shlomo Angel, *Discouraging Crime Through City Planning,* Working Paper #75, (Berkeley: University of California, 1968). Op. cit., Newman.

17. See Presidents Commission on Law Enforcement and Administration of Justice, *Task Force Report: Science and Technology* (Washington, D.C.: U.S. Government Printing Office, 1967): 50.

18. Op. cit., Luedtke, p. 39.

19. John Conklin, *Robbery and the Criminal Justice System* (Philadelphia: J.B. Lippincott Co., 1972), Tables 19 and 20.

Chapter Four

Victimized Persons and Dwellings

INTRODUCTION

Since the differential distribution of burglary rates discussed in Chapter 3 applies not only to whole areas, but also to individual households within areas of comparable rates, the question remains as to why one particular household is burglarized and not another. Some tentative answers to this question were suggested by the target preferences expressed by burglar interviewees and discussed in Chapter 2; but to understand how these preferences may be reflected in actual behavior, one must examine particular targets chosen in the real world. Accordingly, this chapter explores the differences between the people and structures which were and were not victimized in the surveyed areas during the time frame of the study. As noted in Chapter 1, the 18 areas selected for the household survey were stratified according to residential crime rate, income level, racial composition, and predominant housing type to approximate as far as possible a typical large metropolitan area. The survey sample is composed of both a random sample of dwelling units in each of the 18 RAs which had (according to police records) reported a burglary between 1/1/69 and 9/30/71 and a random sample of dwelling units which had *not* reported any burglaries during the same time frame.[a] Throughout most of this chapter, information obtained from the sampling is analyzed according to area crime rate groupings (high,

---

[a] In the following discussion, the number of victimized respondents will not equal the number of victimized dwellings. Fifty-two respondents were interviewed whose homes had been victimized before they moved in but during the time frame of the study. Hence, these 52 respondents were counted as "nonvictims," while their houses were counted as victimized dwellings.

medium and low) to ensure that generalizations will be drawn from persons and structures with relatively "equal" chances of being victimized.[b]

For purposes of establishing socioeconomic characteristics, behavioral traits and attitudes of victims of residential crimes, 125 victims of the randomly sampled reported burglaries were interviewed, and an additional 95 victims of unreported burglaries for which records were not available were also discovered and interviewed during the course of the survey. Thus, a total of 220 victims of residential burglary were interviewed, several of whom had sustained more than one burglary or attempted burglary over the time period of the study. (The extent of multiple victimization is shown in Appendix D, Table D(2)-1.)

Information obtained from the victim interviews is compared with information obtained from interviews with 682 'nonvictims' of residential burglary. Findings are presented in terms of victimization rate (number of individual households victimized per thousand), burglary incidence (total number of burglaries per thousand households), and percent of multiple victimization. Rates and percentages are based on weighted figures to correct for sampling variations,[c] but unweighted numbers (which appear as "*ns*" in tables) are also presented to provide perspective on the weighted figures.

Data was also obtained from the household survey on structural characteristics of victimized dwellings in a form similar to that described above. The information presented was tested for statistical significance with chi square computations, and findings termed significant are so at the .05 level.

VICTIMS

Socioeconomic Characteristics

Income characteristics. The relationship between an individual's income level and the likelihood that he will become a victim of crime was explored in a 1967 National Opinion Research Center (NORC) study, which found that victimization fell most heavily on low income and nonwhite populations. The NORC fingings for burglary in particular, which are presented in Table 4-1, indicate that among whites, victimization rates declined as income rose, whereas among blacks, rates rose with income.

---

[b]The classifications of high, middle, and low crime areas were based on police records and, as noted in Chapter 1, the victimization survey cast doubt on police records for RA 196 and RA 447, both of which were classed as low-crime, but in fact appeared to have sustained a sufficient amount of unreported crime to merit their reclassification as high-crime areas. Consequently, the classification "low crime" frequently appears suspect in the tables for this chapter. Similar deviations appeared, but not so consistently, in areas classed as medium and high crime rate; but the classifications have nevertheless been maintained, since the deviations did not appear sufficient to impair the overall usefulness of the groupings.

[c]See Appendix D(1), for a description of the weighting procedure.

Table 4–1. Distribution of Residential Crime by Race and Income (rates per 100,000 population)

	White				Nonwhite		
Crime	$0-$2,999	$3,000-$5,999	$6,000-$9,999	Above $10,000	$0-$2,999	$3,000-$5,999	Above $6,000
Burglary	1,310	958	764	763	1,336	1,261	2,056

Source: Phillip H. Ennis, *Criminal Victimization in the United States* (Chicago: National Opinion Research Center, 1967), Table 14.

The trend depicted in Table 4-1, however, runs counter to the findings of the victimization survey conducted for the present study, which indicated that victimization rates rise with income among both whites and nonwhites. These findings are summarized in Table 4-2.

Table 4–2. Burglary Victimization by Race and Income*

	V. rate	(n)	Burglary Incidence	% Multiply-Victimized
Black				
Less than $8,000	110	(167)	160	45%
$8,000-$14,999	220	(67)	230	5%
$15,000 or more	270	(36)	500	85%
White				
Less than $8,000	90	(256)	130	44%
$8,000-$14,999	110	(153)	120	9%
$15,000 or more	190	(123)	200	5%
		(802)		

*Differences in group rates significant at .05 level.

The low, middle, and high income definitions in the above table approximate those used by the Bureau of Labor Statistics as standards for a family of four in Boston, and according to these definitions, 53 percent of the sample population were classed as low income in 1971, 26 percent as middle income, and 21 percent as high income. As is apparent from Table 4-2, the most frequently victimized group was the high income black group ($N = 36$) who were also most frequently multiply-victimized. The order is, in terms of decreasing victimization, high income blacks, middle income blacks, high income whites, middle income whites, and low income blacks (same rate, although the incidence figures are higher for the black group), and low income whites.

Victimization rates and income level were also tabulated according to area crime rate groupings, and, as is shown in Table 4-3, the pattern of increasing victimization with increasing income persisted in both high and middle crime RAs:

Table 4-3. Burglary Victimization by Income in Low, Middle, and High Crime RAs*

	V. rate	(N)	Burglary Incidence	% Multiply-Victimized
HC RAs				
Less than $8,000	100	(167)	150	50%
$8,000-$14,999	180	(60)	210	17%
$15,000 or more	250	(40)	370	48%
MC RAs				
Less than $8,000	100	(117)	150	50%
$8,000-$14,999	220	(71)	220	–
$15,000 or more	260	(78)	300	15%
LC RAs				
Less than $8,000	120	(139)	120	–
$8,000-$14,999	60	(89)	60	–
$15,000 or more	110	(41)	120	9%

*Differences in high and middle crime groups significant at the .05 level.

Thus, although the high crime areas are all low-average income areas, the upper income households within both these areas and middle crime areas appear to be victimized most frequently. This pattern does not appear to hold in low crime areas,[d] but does hold overall, when area crime rate groupings are removed. The overall income/victimization pattern is summarized in Table 4-4:

Table 4-4. Burglary Victimization by Income*

	V. rate	(n)	Burglary Incidence	% Multiply-Victimized
Less than $8,000	100	(423)	140	40%
$8,000-$14,999	130	(220)	140	8%
$15,000 or more	190	(159)	230	21%

*Differences in group rates significant at the .05 level.

In spite of the fact that these results are inconsistent with the previously noted findings of the NORC study regarding victimization of whites, the results were to some extent anticipated by the discussion of offender behavior in Chapter 2, which noted the propensity of burglars to select the more affluent among available targets. The results were also partially anticipated by the discussion of income and burglary rates in Chapter 3, which concluded that, while low-income areas were generally more likely to display high rates, rates

[d]The low-crime areas include two RAs—196 and 447—where the low reported rates are suspect. Since both these areas are lower income, their presence in the low-crime group may cause the deviation from income/victimization pattern for the group.

tended to increase with income in suburban areas and predominantly black areas. These conflicting patterns were attributed to the separate operations of income as a factor in the formation of a criminal population and income as a factor in the criminal's selection of targets. That is, while a low-average income level appeared to contribute to the determination of the criminal population present in a high crime area and hence to the area's overall crime rate, a high income level may contribute to the attractiveness of the area as a target.

For all these reasons, the correlation of increasing victimization with increasing income does not seem illogical. However, the disagreement between the findings of the present study and those of the NORC study regarding victimization of whites remains troublesome. Whether this disagreement is attributable to some as yet unidentified idiosyncrasy of the Boston area, or to some hidden bias in the samples used for either of the studies, cannot be determined within the confines of this book; but in noting the disagreement, one should also note that the NORC survey was conducted nationwide and the present survey in one large metropolitan area. It may be, then, that the victimization of the relatively affluent by the relatively poor occurs most consistently in urban areas like Boston, where affluent and poor live in close proximity. Such a pattern might not appear in smaller towns and rural areas, where populations are spatially less concentrated and economically more homogeneous.

Race.   Although the preceding discussion noted that high income blacks evidenced the highest victimization rate of any population group, Table 4-5 indicates that, overall, no significant differences in victimization existed between the blacks and whites.

Table 4-5.   Victimization by Race in Low, Middle, and High Crime RAs*

	V. rate	(n)	Burglary Incidence	% Multiply-Victimized
HC RAs				
Black	90	(161)	140	55%
White	140	(132)	210	50%
MC RAs				
Black	210	(83)	280	33%
White	170	(187)	180	6%
LC RAs				
Black	140	(50)	220	57%
White	70	(285)	90	29%
		(898)		

*Differences in high crime areas only are significant at the .05 level.

Although blacks in general were victimized only slightly more often than whites, they did tend to be multiply-victimized much more often (see Appendix D, Table D(2)-2). Also, blacks in middle and low crime areas, where they constitute a relatively small percentage of the total population, were victimized more often than whites, but the reverse was true in high crime areas, where blacks averaged 55 percent of the population. (See Appendix D, Table D(2)-3.)

Age and Marital Status. As indicated in Table 4-6, victims tended to be significantly younger than nonvictims:

Table 4-6. Victimization Rate by Age of Head of Household*

	V. rate	(n)
30 years or less	230	(319)
31-64 years	150	(406)
65 or more years	90	(138)
		(863)

*Differences in group rates significant at the .05 level.

These findings are consistent with police data on burglary victims in the surveyed areas, which indicate that 44 percent of the households victimized were headed by someone between the ages of 21 and 30 and only 5 percent, by someone over 65. (See Appendix D, Table D(2)-4.)

Moreover, single persons, particularly young single persons, were significantly more likely to be victimized than were married persons of any age (see Appendix D, Table D(2)-5). The high victimization rates for the young and single and the low rates for the elderly appear largely attributable to the occupancy patterns discussed in this chapter; since burglary generally occurs on unoccupied premises and since elderly and married people appear to spend more time in their homes than do the young and single, the former are less likely to become victims of residential burglars.

Education and Occupation. Although Table 4-7 below indicates increasing victimization with increasing level of education, this tendency did not prove statistically significant.

Table 4-7. Victimization by Education of Head of Household

	V. Rate	(n)
Less than grade 12	210	(284)
High school graduate	270	(253)
Any college	310	(265)
Higher degree	430	(95)
		(897)

Also, professional persons appeared to be victimized slightly more often than were nonprofessionals, but again, these findings did not prove significant. (See Appendix D, Table D(2)-6.) It seems probable then, that the minor association noted in the survey between education/occupation levels and burglary victimization is more attributable to the correlation of these two factors with income than to any intrinsic quality of the factors themselves.

Behavioral Characteristics of Victims and Nonvictims

Occupancy Behavior. Since the tendency of burglaries to occur on unoccupied premises has been noted elsewhere in this book, the household survey anticipated that individuals who left their homes unoccupied for substantial portions of time would experience significantly greater victimization than those who spent relatively more time at home. As indicated by Table 4-8, this anticipation was confirmed:

Table 4-8. Victimization by Occupancy Pattern*

	V. Rate	(n)	Burglary Incidence	% Multiply-Victimized
Out 0-5 daytime hours per week	80	(372)	100	25%
Out 5-35 hours per week	140	(262)	160	14%
Out more than 35 hours per week	160	(230) (864)	220	38%

*Differences in group rates significant at .05 level. The same pattern held when occupancy was evaluated on a daily, rather than weekly, basis (See appendix D, Table D(2)-7.)

Social Isolation. The relationship between the social cohesion of an area and its crime rate was discussed in some detail in Chapter 3, and a rough index derived to measure variations in cohesion from area to area. To measure the relative "isolation" of individual victims and nonvictims within the surveyed areas, the same three questions used to measure area cohesion were applied to individuals—but with much less coherent results. As indicated in Table 4-9, no significant relationship appears between an individual's 'isolation' and the probability of his being victimized—although the isolated were victimized and multiply victimized slightly more often than their numbers in the sample population would merit. However, a significant relationship between victimization and social isolation did exist in the low burglary rate RAs (see Appendix D, Table D(2)-8), where victimization and particularly multiple-victimization rose

Table 4–9. Victimization by Social Isolation*

	V. Rate	(n)	Incidence
Isolated	140	(289)	200
Somewhat isolated	100	(403)	130
Not isolated	120	(210)	130
		(902)	

*Not statistically significant at the .05 level.

the more a person was isolated from his neighbors. As the low crime RAs in general exhibited the most cohesion, an individual's isolation from his neighbors in these areas may simply be more apparent to a prospective burglar, particularly if the latter is a resident of the area. Data also indicated, however, that in low crime RAs (only) isolation was related to being away from home frequently, so that the higher victimization rates may be more attributable to occupancy behavior than to isolation *per se.*

Awareness of Crime. To obtain some general understanding of the association between an individual's fear of victimization and his actual experience, members of the sample population were asked:

> How worried are you about your home being broken into or entered illegally when no one is at home? Would you say *very worried, somewhat worried, just a little worried,* or *not worried at all*?

Responses were ranked high or low according to the level of fear expressed, and as indicated in Table 4-10, the experience of victimization appeared significantly associated with fear.

Table 4–10. Victimization by Fear of Being Victimized*

	V. Rate	(N)
High fear level	350	(436)
Low fear level	120	(427)
		(863)

Seventy-three percent of the victims in all the RAs expressed considerable fear, compared to 41 percent of the nonvictims; but the relationship between fear and victimization was most conspicuous in the low crime RAs, where in general people seem the least worried. Also, 57 percent of the female respondents expressed considerable fear, as compared with only 31 percent of the males.

The relationship between victimization, sex, and fear was also noted by the President's Commission Report, from which Table 4-11 was taken:

Table 4–11. Concern of Victims and Nonvictims About Burglary and Robbery (in percentages)

Worry about Burglary or Robbery	*Victim*	*Nonvictim*
Males:		
Worried	69%	59%
Not worried	31	41
	100%	100%
Number of males	(1,456)	(3,930)
Females:		
Worried	84%	77%
Not worried	16	23
	100%	100%
Number of females	(2,399)	(6,189)

Source: Task Force Report: *Crime and its Impact—An Assessment* (Washington: U.S. Government Printing Office, 1967), p. 86.

As regards the relationship between fear and race, the present study found that blacks appeared significantly more fearful than whites. Sixty-nine percent of the blacks and 40 percent of the whites said they were either "very" or "somewhat" worried, and within the "worried" category, 45 percent of the blacks were "very worried" while only 21 percent of the whites felt comparably strongly. Finally, 31 percent of the white respondents and 17 percent of the blacks said they were "not at all worried."

As is apparent from Table 4-12, these findings are somewhat similar to those of the NORC victimization study mentioned previously.

Table 4–12. Concern About Burglary

	White		Nonwhite	
Response	*Male*	*Female*	*Male*	*Female*
Very concerned	11%	14%	22%	25%
Somewhat concerned	36	38	29	37
Not worried	53	48	49	38
Total	100%	100%	100%	100%
	(4,668)	(7,515)	(646)	(1,037)

Source: Phillip H. Ennis, *Victimization of Crime in the United States* (Chicago: National Opinion Research Center, 1967), Table 46.

Finally, no significant correlation could be found between fear and either income level or distance of residence from the city core, although residents of public housing projects appeared consistently more fearful than other members of the survey population.

All of the above observations lead to the conclusion that although the experience of victimization and the residential burglary rate of an area appear associated with an individual resident's feeling of fear, these factors seem to be only partial explanations of the uneven distribution of fear within the population studied. Of the four RAs with the highest overall fear levels (256, 196, 736, and 291) two are medium crime areas, one a high-crime housing project, and one a housing project where the police records indicate a low rate but survey responses indicate it may actually be a high rate area (196). Victims in these four RAs were not significantly more afraid than nonvictims, which suggests that the high level of fear in these areas may be more attributable to some intangible "atmosphere" than to any actual experience with burglary. It would, however, be very difficult to determine what kind of 'atmosphere' the areas might have in common, since two of the areas are housing projects (196 white, 256 black), one is a suburban area with median income above $28,000 (736) and one a lower income area of small multifamily homes occupied by a population whose racial composition is rapidly becoming more black (291).

In any case, victimization experience did appear to have some effect on security behavior, as well as an effect on fear level. Forty-three percent of the victims—as opposed to 19 percent of the nonvictims—indicated that they had changed their security practices during the past year, and the majority attributed the change to the experience of being burglarized. Table 4-13 presents the victimization rates for those who did and did not alter their security practices and Appendix D, Table D(2)-9 lists the specific measures taken by the survey sample.

Table 4-13.   Victimization by Security Practice Change*

	V. rate	(n)	Burglary Incidence	% Multiply-Victimized
Has changed	260	(230)	310	19%
Has not changed	70	(672)	100	43%
		(902)		

*Differences in group rates significant at .05 level.

VICTIMIZED STRUCTURES

This section focuses on the possible relationship between a dwelling unit's physical characteristics and its probability of being burglarized. The characteristics to be analyzed fall into two basic categories, the first relating to the accessibility of the structure (the number and type of potential entry portals—doors and windows—and the quality of portal security—locks, construction, etc.) and the second relating to the possibilities of detection (the visibility of the portals to persons in neighboring dwelling units and/or on the street, the use of burglar alarms, dogs, etc). Predictably, however, analysis of detection (visibility) and access factors is complicated by their interactive nature. Visibility factors, for example, may lessen the number of potential portals available to the burglar, since, clearly, unconventional entry through a vulnerable front window in full view of the street and neighboring houses would generally be less preferable to a burglar than entry through a more physically secure but less visible back door. Portal visibility can also alter the absolute level of portal security by affecting the duration and/or method of attack, since the more visible the portal, the more quickly it must be violated. Similarly, very low portal security will virtually nullify the deterrent effect of visibility. Finally, the relative weight of both access and detection factors will be influenced by the various factors discussed in previous chapters: most particularly, by the skill level of the attacking burglar, the occupancy patterns of the residents, and the social organization of the neighborhood.

In addition to analyzing access and detection factors, this section also examines the distribution of "standard" door security by geographic location, type of structure, income of household, etc., and summarizes the nature of the deficiencies causing most doors to be rated "nonstandard." As described in the introduction to this chapter, the sample upon which all of the following analyses are based was randomly drawn from dwellings within the 18 surveyed RAs. No luxury high-rise buildings were included in the survey, but since Chapter 3 established that these structures display uniformly high levels of security and low burglary rates, no bias to the sample was anticipated from their exclusion. The sampled dwellings are summarized in Table 4-14.

Table 4–14. Distribution of Types of Structure in Sample

	Single Family		Small Multiunit (2-9 units)		Large Multiunit (10+)		Public		Private	
	%	(N)	%	(N)	%	(N)	%	(N)	%	(N)
All RAs	25%	(168)	40%	(432)	35%	(234)	24%	(148)	76%	(686)
High crime	9%	(31%)	40%	(153)	51%	(78)	44%	(52)	56%	(210)
Middle crime	26%	(67%)	40%	(121)	34%	(93)	22%	(52)	78%	(229)
Low crime	32%	(67%)	40%	(158)	28%	(63)	15%	(44)	85%	(247)

Access Factors

Number of Portals. As is indicated in Table 4-15, the probability of a dwelling units being burglarized tends to increase with the number of entry options available to the burglar—particularly when these options include windows as well as doors:

Table 4-15. Burglary Incidence Rates by Number of Doors Leading Directly to the Dwelling Unit With and Without Accessible Windows

	1 Door		*1 Door Windows*		*2 Doors*		*2 Doors Windows*		*3 Doors*		*3 Doors Windows*	
	Rate	*(N)*	*Rate*	*(N)*	*Rate*	*(N)*	*Rate*	*(N)*	*Rate*	*(N)*	*Rate*	*(N)*
All RAs*	74	(50)	166	(153)	179	(104)	176	(126)	116	(115)	194	(153)
High crime*	66	(11)	169	(38)	80	(36)	400	(45)	95	(59)	409	(47)
Middle crime*	169	(24)	303	(54)	57	(44)	211	(37)	49	(26)	279	(34)
Low crime	10	(15)	66	(61)	365	(24)	45	(44)	258	(30)	77	(72)

*Denotes statistical significance at the .05 level.

Although the pattern is sporadic in middle and low crime areas, it is conspicuously consistent in the high crime areas, where the presence of accessible windows appears to have a clear and strong effect on a unit's 'victimizability.' That the trend would appear more consistent in high crime areas than elsewhere was partially anticipated by the offender behavior data presented in Chapter 2, which indicated that young unskilled burglars—those most prevalent in high crime areas—tend to value accessibility of structure more highly than any other target characteristic.

Although Table 4-15 does not show a strong connection between burglary incidence and number of doors leading to individual dwelling units, a strong connection did appear between burglary incidence and number of doors leading *into* small multiunit buildings. Table 4-16 documents the connection:

Table 4-16. Burglary Rates in Multifamily Structures for Units Without Accessible Windows by Number of Doors Leading into the Structure

	1 Door		*2 Doors*		*3 Doors*	
	Rate	*(N)*	*Rate*	*(N)*	*Rate*	*(N)*
All RAs*						
Small multiunit	63	(42)	153	(89)	474	(23)
Large multiunit	128	(76)	86	(34)	0	(6)

*Denotes statistical significance at the .05 level.

(Single family homes were removed from the sample, since they almost universally have accessible windows.)

In fact, as is suggested by Table 4-16, small multiunit buildings appear to have a higher victimization probability than other types of housing,[e] which is not surprising in view of the fact that these structures display the security disadvantages of both single-family homes (which have multiple access points) and large multiunit buildings (which have interior nonvisible doors to dwelling units.

Standard and Nonstandard Doors. In order to measure the door security of individual dwelling units, the household survey ranked doors as "standard" or "nonstandard" according to a system somewhat more stringent than Federal Crime Insurance requirements, but less so than the proposed Federal Security Code.[1] For purposes of this study, a standard door must (1) be of metal, metal panels, solid wood, or hollow wood of three-quarter inch thickness; (2) have no unprotected glass near the door handle; (3) have no exposed hinges; (4) lock with either a three-quarter inch dead latch or dead bolt or a vertical bolt.

Only the doors leading directly to the dwelling unit were evaluated, and, since the evaluation sought to determine the effectiveness of standard doors, burglaries through windows and attempted burglaries were removed from the sample. Nevertheless, a few doors were entered without actually being 'defeated'— i.e., because a key was used or a door was left unlocked.

The quantity of standard doors in the sample was low: only 8 percent of the units had all standard doors, and only 4 percent now had at least one standard door. The 8 percent of the sample dwelling units which were protected by standard doors were unevenly distributed both geographically and socially, with the highest percentage located in the inner city. Also, 15 percent of the units in large multiunit structures were protected, 6 percent in small multiunit, 4 percent in single family attached, and none in single family separate homes. Finally, households earning less than $8,000 appeared better protected than higher income households, but this greater level of protection among lower income groups appears chiefly attributable to public housing, which accounts for the majority of protected units in the lower income category. (Approximately 18 percent of the public housing units were protected, versus 5 percent of the private units.)

Among the remaining 92 percent of dwelling units, 39 percent of the doors were classed nonstandard because they were constructed of wood panel, 26 percent because they had glass near the door handle, 8 percent because of removable exterior hinges, and the remainder because of inadequate locking systems. (In fact, most of nonstandard doors had multiple defects.)

---

[e]Victimization rates for each type of dwelling unit are as follows:
Dwelling units in—

	Rate	*(N)*
Small multiunit structures:	185	(432)
Large multiunit structures:	142	(234)

In spite of the small number of standard doors in the sample, burglary incidence did appear inversely related to standard door security, although significantly only in middle crime areas:

Table 4–17. Burglary Incidence Rate Through Door by Door Vulnerability in High, Middle, and Low Crime RAs

	Nonstandard Doors		All Standard Doors	
	Rate	*(N)*	*Rate*	*(N)*
All RAs	81	(830)	28	(57)
High crime	105	(273)	17	(27)
Middle crime*	98	(275)	44	(25)
Low crime	55	(283)	24	(5)

*Denotes statistical significance at the .05 level.

The fact that the burglary rates against units with nonstandard doors are particularly high in high and middle crime areas suggests that standard doors may be more effective precautions against burglary in areas victimized primarily by the young and unskilled than elsewhere.

In order to test the independence of the door variable from other factors already established to be influential on burglary rates, the door variable was tabulated according to both occupancy patterns and income level. The results, contained in Appendix D, Tables D(2)-10 and 11, generally confirmed independent influence of door quality on burglary rate.

Detection Factors

Since the offender interviews suggested that, next to actual occupancy of the dwelling unit, burglars were most often deterred by the presence of neighbors or other possible witnesses, it seems probable that most burglars would prefer to enter dwelling units through the least conspicuous portals. While a door is obviously the most conventional way of entering a dwelling, it is also the easiest to secure, and consequently, the burglar has a tradeoff between the 'detectibility' of a window entrance and the relative 'inaccessibility' of the door. Of the 172 surveyed cases which offered both window and door options, the door was preferred in 61 percent of the cases, as indicated in Table 4-18.

Since, in those cases where a window option was selected, entry would presumably be less noticeable on the side or rear of the dwelling than on the front, it was not surprising to find that, of 79 window attacks, three-quarters were made against a side or rear window.

Also, previous research has suggested that corner structures may have a higher probability of being burglarized than others, since the lack of an

Table 4–18. Portal Attacked When Choice of Door or Window by Structure Type

Structure Type	Door %	Door (N)	Window %	Window (N)	Total %	Total (N)
Single family	67%	(36)	33%	(18)	100%	(54)
Small multiunit	58%	(48)	42%	(35)	100%	(83)
Large multinuit	60%	(21)	40%	(14)	100%	(35)
Totals	61%	(105)	39%	(67)	100%	(172)

adjacent structure would not only reduce detection possibilities but would also expand entry-exit opportunities.[2] The higher rate of corner structures was in fact confirmed by the household survey data presented in Table 4-19.

Table 4–19. Burglary By Location on Block and Structure Type

Structure Type*	Corner Rate	Corner (N)	Noncorner Rate	Noncorner (N)
Single family	253	(30)	109	(141)
Small multiunit	194	(62)	185	(373)
Large multiunit	273	(28)	122	(206)
Total	242	(120)	144	(720)

*Denotes statistical significance at the .05 level.

Finally, no evaluation could be made of the effectiveness of such other detection measures as burglar alarms and dogs, since two few of the households surveyed possessed either. However, in the context of a discussion of crime control strategies, the following chapter does employ information obtained from the offender interviews to arrive at some tentative assessment of the effectiveness of common detection measures.

NOTES

1. Federal Crime Insurance Program of National Housing Act as amended by P.L. 91-609. *Federal Security Code with Minimum Building Security Guidelines and Cost Estimates for the Security Features* (Initial Draft) of the National Institute of Law Enforcement and Criminal Justice, Law Enforcement Assistance Administration, May 14, 1971.

2. See Gerald Luedtke and Associates, *Crime and the Physical City* (Detroit: by the author, 1970) 36.

Chapter Five

Control of Residential Crime

INTRODUCTION

The preceding chapters have examined the problem of residential crime in terms of three components—the offender, his environment, and his victim. Using observations from those chapters and other information gathered from the offender interviews and household surveys, Chapter 5 evaluates the policy implications of this study for the control of residential crime.

Crime control strategies may be broadly divided into two categories: those which aim at absolute reduction in the number of offenders and/or their frequency of operation, and those which aim at a reduction in the opportunities open to the offenders. Obviously, strategies of the first category—if effective and not prohibitive in social or economic costs—would be ultimately the most preferable, since they circumvent the serious problem of displacement inherent in the second category. That is, programs which aim only at foreclosing criminal opportunity while leaving the criminal population intact run the grave risk of simply transferring the population from one area to another or from one type of crime to another, since it seems clearly impossible to arrive at an absolutely uniform foreclosure of opportunity for every conceivable kind of crime. The problem of displacement does not usually arise among programs aimed at reducing the offender population; but needless to say, such programs appear extremely difficult to implement with any success. Altering the environment in which a criminal operates will likely prove a simpler matter than altering the behavior of individual criminals or the forces which produce criminal populations.

The present study was not equipped to undertake a sociopsychological analysis of interviewed offenders and, consequently, cannot evaluate with any precision the possible approaches to the alteration of criminal behavior. Nevertheless, some tentative observations on this subject can be drawn from the offender interview data presented in this chapter. The remaining sections deal with the role of the criminal justice system, the community, and specific environmental factors in foreclosing opportunities for residential crime.

OFFENDER BEHAVIOR

Among the various factors analyzed in Chapter 2 in connection with offender behavior, the factor of drug use appears most strongly correlated with recent increases in residential crime in the Boston area. From 1962 to 1970, Boston's residential burglary and robbery rates rose by 340 and 920 percent respectively, yet the sexual composition of the population remained virtually unchanged; black population only rose from 10-16 percent, the youth population by less than 5 percent, and the median income for both whites and nonwhites rose steadily.[1] During the same period, the number of heoin addicts in the Boston area was estimated to have increased by a factor of ten, and narcotic drug arrests increased from 149 to 2,106.[2] Apparent increases in drug use have paralleled increases in residential crime to such an extent that a relationship between the two can be logically inferred. Further support for this inference can be derived from the offender interview data presented in Chapter 2, which indicated that drug users tend to operate with much greater frequency than nondrug users.

It seems probable, then, that if drug-users were to be cured, or their habit met in some way that did not require them to steal, a major drop in the Boston residential burglary rates would ensue. Even if the drug-users continued to steal, the rates would still go down as the frequency of their activity diminished. Assuming the interviewee population is representative, if the drug-using offenders reduced their level of activity to that of their non-drug-using criminal counterparts, the offender interview data indicates that Boston would experience a 20 percent reduction in its annual residential burglary rates. Were the drug-users to cease operations altogether, the reduction would amount to 50 percent. Whether an individual's use of drugs or whether the current cultural and legal treatment of the drug-using individual are susceptible to social change remain questions outside the scope of the present report. Suffice it to note, however, that some such change would appear extremely productive to programs aimed at controlling residential crimes.

As regards control of the non-drug-using criminal, little can be suggested in the context of the present study. It did appear to the research staff that the offenders interviewed for this study were not, by and large, "philosophical" criminals; that is, they appeared to have no particular commitment to crime per se, but rather were individuals who met certain needs by engaging in criminal behavior and who might be equally content to meet these needs in a noncriminal way, if such an alternative was available to them. In a sense, the choice of a criminal career appears logical for many of the interviewees, given their consumption preferences and the legitimate options open to them to satisfy those preferences. Burglary, after all, did appear to offer a relatively good return for independent work and little tedium—vocational benefits hard to attain for the relatively unskilled and uneducated. Although the prospect of imprisonment might seem discouraging, offenders seem to be seldom caught relative to the number of crimes they commit, and an occasional brief period in jail does not appear to discourage many offenders.

These observations suggest very tentatively that rehabilitation programs might best be aimed not at altering the offenders' moral values—which do not appear easily alterable over short periods of time and under programs of diffused focus—but rather, at helping them to duplicate their "working situation" in some legitimate occupation. Construction work, for example, offers rewards somewhat similar to burglary: good pay, relative choice as to amount of labor and duration of commitment, and some of the challenge associated with the exercise of physical skills.

Finally, it should be noted that no single approach to "rehabilitation" can be expected to meet the needs and peculiarities of all types of burglars. The younger burglar, for example, who steals with his friends as much for fun as for profit, might be diverted from his activities by some organized group program that the older burglar (with his harder profit motive) would find irrelevant and uninteresting. Although the example is much simplified, the point is fundamental; programs which aim at controlling criminal behavior must be appropriate to the specific type of criminal whose behavior is at issue. Even if appropriate, such programs may have little likelihood of success, but if inappropriate, they are probably useless.

THE CRIMINAL JUSTICE SYSTEM

Police

The problems encountered by the police in attempting to control residential crime were noted briefly in Chapter 3, which attributed the very low arrest rate for residential crimes to their low visibility. However, the potential role of the police in countering these crimes may be circumscribed not only by the nature of the crimes themselves, but also by the limitations of standard police operating procedures.

In brief, police departments generally rely on a strategy of "detection, deterrence, and apprehension" (DDA) to counteract criminal activity.[3] The strategy involves:

1. *Omnipresence:* An attempt to project to the maximum extent a belief on the part of potential offenders in the likelihood of police presence at any given point in time and space.
2. *Aggressive patrol:* An attempt to interdict crime by locating and challenging suspicious persons.
3. *Rapid response:* The capability of quickly responding to emergency calls in order that criminals may be apprehended in the act.
4. *Follow-up investigation:* Use of investigative techniques which maximize the possibility that the offenders who are successful in fleeing from crimes will be apprehended at a later date.

Although well-established in standard texts on police administration, the crime control techniques outlined above have been the subject of some controversy in recent research—particularly as these techniques are applied to property offenders. A Washington, D.C. study, for example, revealed that an interview sample of convicted felons (mostly robbers and burglars) did not in general accurately perceive the size and nature of police operations, and took few precautions against the possibility of police interference in their crimes. The study concluded that either offenders were not very rational and simply not fearful of the consequences, or else, that they were able to block out the fear. The study also found that burglars were the least susceptible to police deterrence, since (it was hypothesized) they worked in the lowest visibility situations.[4]
Similar findings emerged from a study of robbery offenders in the Boston area, which concluded that one-third of the interviewed sample did not consider the possibility of capture, one-third consciously blocked out the fear, and one-third thought that chances of capture were minimal.[5]

These findings are fairly consistent with the offender interview data presented in Chapter 2 and in Appendix E, Table E-1. Only 14 percent of the interviewees indicated that they were even interested in determining the presence of police patrols prior to making a hit;[a] approximately 50 percent of the interviewees indicated that patrols, even if apparent, would have no effect on their decision to hit a particular target; only 14 percent indicated that clear evidence of patrols would definitely deter them, while the remaining interviewees left the question open.

The relative disregard of the interviewees for police patrols appears largely justified by the low arrest rates for burglary noted in Chapter 3. The arrest index for burglary in the 39 areas surveyed for this study was calculated at .04 (see Table 3-13), which means that only four out of every 100 burglaries resulted in arrests. Given the large number of unreported crimes, the true arrest figure is probably substantially lower.

---

[a]See Appendix B, Table B(2)-9.

These findings approximate those of a Rand Institute study of police apprehension activities in the New York area, which determined that the probability of arrest differs vastly between what the study called crimes of passion (homicide, rape, assault), and crimes of profit (robbery, burglary, larceny). The Rand study also found that the vast majority of arrests for property crimes were made near the scene of the crime or as a result of evidence that was readily apparent at the time the crime was reported. For property crimes not resulting in fairly prompt arrest, the probability of eventual arrest through detective investigation was found to be extremely low—.06 for robbery, .02 for larceny, and .01 for burglary. In contrast to crimes of passion, the probability of arrest for crimes of profit does not appear to increase substantially if more effort is devoted to the case.[6]

All these observations cast doubt on the efficacy of the DDA strategy as applied to common crimes against property, which constitute the bulk of all residential crimes. First of all, the police technique of appearing omnipresent seems to have little effect on the majority of residential offenders who either do not perceive the "omnipresence" of the police or simply do not fear it. Secondly, the technique of aggressive patrol seems ineffective against crimes which generally take place out of view of patrolling police. Third, the effort to respond rapidly to emergency calls seems irrelevant to crimes like burglary, the vast majority of which are committed on unoccupied premises and not discovered until sometime after they are committed. Finally, the apparent failure of follow-up investigation in leading to arrests is not very surprising—at least for burglary cases, where there are generally no witnesses and no traceable links between offender and victim.

Finally, of course, police are limited in their ability to counteract residential crimes simply by their numbers—by the ratio of police resources to possible targets and by the competing demands of other tasks on police resources (see Table 5-1). As is apparent from Table 5-1, sworn police manpower in the Boston area has increased by less than 10 percent between 1962 and 1970, while reported crimes more than doubled, and total calls for service increased by at least 70 percent.

One fact, however, which balances the seemingly bleak showing of the police in controlling residential crime is that most offenders commit multiple offenses over a period of time and are, therefore, quite likely to be caught at some point in their career. Although it is possible that a large number of property offenders never surface in police arrest records, this possibility seems remote in view of the findings of the present study. In the city of Boston, for example, approximately 1,000 people were arrested for burglary in 1970, while approximately 10,000 burglaries were reported to the police. If we assume that the actual number of burglaries was approximately three times the reported number, and also assume that the number of persons arrested roughly coincides with the size of actual burglar population in the area, then each burglar operating

Table 5-1. Representative Indicators of Boston Police Work Load, 1962-1970

Year	Total Calls for Service	Part I Offenses*	Sworn Police Manpower
1962	NA	20,515	2,595
1963	NA	20,612	2,557
1964	199,172	22,517	2,572
1965	220,847	26,132	2,495
1966	229,741	25,806	2,513
1967	236,475	28,215	2,494
1968	286,784	36,452	2,617
1969	332,458	39,942	2,607
1970	340,742	43,335	2,805

*Part I offenses include criminal homicide, forcible rape, robbery, aggravated assault, burglary, larceny, and auto theft.

Source: *Annual Report, Boston Police Department, 1970,* Figure 1.

independently would average only 30 burglaries a year, or about one every two weeks. If we assume that the burglars operate in groups of at least two (which assumption seems merited on the basis of the offender interview data), then 500 two-men teams would average 60 burglaries per year ($\frac{30,000}{500}$) for an income of $3,000 per individual ($60 \times \frac{\$100}{2}$).[b] To posit a burglar population substantially larger than the arrested population would, then, require an assumption that large numbers of burglars work only infrequently and not primarily for economic gain[c]—which assumption cannot be justified in the context of the present study. Indeed, the information on frequency of operation obtained from the offender interviewees (see Appendix B, Table B(2)-17) suggested that the interviewees were responsible for many more crimes than their police records indicated.

Courts and Correctional Institutions

If the burglar population is in fact—as it appears from the foregoing discussion—relatively small[d] and known to the police through repeated arrests, then responsibility for the "control" of the criminal behavior of this population would seem to rest more with the courts and correctional system than with the local police departments. Even if police procedures were somehow altered to permit an increase in the arrest index for residential crimes, it seems improbable

---

[b]As noted in Chapter 2, the average gain from a residential burglary is only about $100.

[c]If, for example, the actual burglar population were assumed to be five times the size of the arrested population, the average annual gain of each burglar operation individually would amount to only $600 ($\frac{30,000}{5,000} \times \$100 = \$600$).

[d]In Boston, on the order of 1,000 out of 70,000 males between the ages of 14 and 24 and much smaller for other population groups.

that any substantial drop would result in the rate at which these crimes are committed, since the median sentence for the crime of burglary is only six months, and apparently, very few burglars decide to switch to a legitimate career during the period of their incarceration.

An increase in the arrest index, then, might simply mean that the police were arresting (for the most part) the same people slightly more often. The probability that this would occur can be appreciated from a brief examination of disposition of most burglary cases after arrests have been made.

In Massachusetts most persons charged with a burglary type offense are tried at the district court level. Although the district courts technically cannot dispose of breaking and entering cases where the penalty is more than ten years imprisonment, most burglary cases are in fact handled at this level (78 percent in 1970), since the police prosecutor will generally reduce the charge to one which the district court can hear. (The reduction of charge usually occurs when the defendant has agreed to plead guilty in return for a lesser sentence.) Defendants found guilty at district court level may be fined, given a suspended sentence, placed on probation, or sentenced—juveniles to the youth service division and adults to the house of correction (a medium security penal institution operated by county government).

Alternatively, the district court judge or the district attorney may elect to send a case to the grand jury for indictment and subsequent trial in the superior court, if they feel the defendant's crime or past history merits a state prison sentence. Individuals who are held for the grand jury and indicted, tried, and convicted in the superior court may receive any of the same penalties given in district court or may be sentenced to a term in the state prison. However, the latter penalty is seldom used.

As is apparent from Table 5-2, between 1966 and 1970 the percentage of arrested burglars who were convicted declined, fewer of those convicted were imprisoned, and of those imprisoned, a higher percentage received short terms in houses of correction rather than state prison sentences.

Although Table 5-2 indicates that in 1970 the average Boston area burglar had less chance of being caught, convicted, and incarcerated than in 1966, one cannot conclude from this fact alone that a trend toward liberality in the courts has contributed in any substantial way to the rise in residential burglary rates. Offenders who receive only probation or relatively short sentences may in fact be more likely to forego criminal behavior than those who receive longer prison terms, but no available information is adequate to determine this—and in any case, the question lies outside the scope of the present study. For our purposes, it is sufficient to note that relatively few persons (less than one-fourth) arrested for burglary are actually imprisoned for the crime.

A similar observation can be made of persons arrested for robbery. Although district courts do not have jurisdiction to try robbery cases, they do conduct the preliminary hearings to determine probable cause and often dismiss

Table 5-2. Number of Reported Burglaries and Court Dispositions of Burglary Arrests, Selected Years Boston SMSA

	1966	1968	1970
Number of reported burglaries[a]	19,204	25,332	33,934
Number of persons tried for burglary[b]	1,819	2,218	2,286
Total % convicted	74%	64%	61%
Sentences to imprisonment as % of total cases tried[c]	30%	24%	21%
% of total sentenced to imprisonment who were received at state prison[d]	30%	20%	17%

[a]Source: *FBI, Uniform Crime Reports,* 1966, 1968, 1970.

[b]Does not include pending cases.

[c]Does not include cases pending sentence.

[d]Based on figures for entire state.

Source: *Statistical Reports of the Commissioner of Corrections,* Commonwealth of Massachusetts, 1966, 1968, 1970.

the case or reduce the charge at this stage. Robbery charges not dismissed or reduced for trial in the district court are heard in superior court. Based on the disposition of robbery cases summarized in Table 5-3, it would appear that robbers, in contrast to burglars, are more likely to be tried in superior court, to be imprisoned if convicted, and to be received in maximum security institutions.

Table 5-3. Disposition of Robbery Prosecutions, Boston SMSA 1970

Number of persons tried for robbery[a]	797
Total % convicted	40%
Sentenced to imprisonment as % of total cases tried[b]	27%
% of total sentenced to imprisonment, sentenced to house of correction[c]	10%
% of total sentenced to imprisonment, sentenced to state prison[d]	90%

[a]Does not include pending cases.

[b]Does not include cases pending sentence.

[c]Does not include cases pending sentence.

[d]Based on figures for entire state.

Source: *Statistical Reports of the Commissioner of Corrections,* Commonwealth of Massachusetts, 1970.

However, in spite of the fact that robbers are more likely than burglars to be imprisoned if convicted, they appear less likely to be convicted in the first place, so that the actual proportion of arrests resulting in imprisonment appears roughly the same—about one quarter—for both types of offenders.

These observations suggest two possible approaches to the control of residential crimes by means of the criminal justice system. First, the known offender population could be dealt with more severely by the courts; more repeat offenders could be sent to prison and for longer periods of time, on the rationale that society will sustain one, three, or even five fewer burglaries for every week the offender is in custody. This rationale rests on the assumption that the primary goal of the prison system is neither punishment nor rehabilitation, but simply isolation of the known criminal population. Although the assumption may appear socially unpalatable when stated so baldly, it seems to be the de facto principle governing the present operation of the criminal justice system. That is, although neither criminologists, correctional officials, nor the public at large can agree on the proper treatment of criminal behavior, offenders continue to be sentenced to institutions which are generally conceded to be inadequate for "correctional" purposes, because (presumably) at some point most people do agree that certain individuals simply must be "gotten off the streets." Some more explicit agreement on the aims of "correctional" institutions would clearly enable the criminal justice system to operate with greater consistency and efficiency in countering the current crime problem.

Secondly, specific programs could be instituted to alter offender motivation. Although neither punishment nor rehabilitation—as presently conceived—has been effective in altering motivation to date, part of the problem may lie in the confusion of purpose noted above regarding the aims of the correctional system. Indeed, one Washington, D.C. study concluded that the experience of imprisonment was simply not sufficiently punitive to constitute an effective deterrent to crime, nor sufficiently rehabilitative to rechannel the offenders' interests in a legitimate direction.[7] Conclusions such as these have prompted substantial research and experimentation on the subject of rehabilitation, but, regardless of the current high level of effort in this area, more seems still to be required. The present report, which was not primarily intended as an evaluation of rehabilitation alternatives, can only conclude that more effort is particularly required in designing programs appropriate for the specific types of offenders involved in common residential crimes, and in designing programs whose impact and duration exceed that of the typical jail term.

THE ROLE OF THE COMMUNITY

Partly as a result of the discouraging record of the criminal justice system in dealing with common residential crimes, much interest of late has centered on the potential of individual communities for, in effect, policing themselves. One noticeable consequence of this interest is increased interaction between police departments and the communities they serve through the operations of crime prevention bureaus within municipal police departments. In essence, these bureaus seek to foreclose criminal opportunities by conducting premise surveys aimed at identifying target vulnerabilities, providing public education programs, and assisting in the design of building security codes.[8] One such program, operated by the police department and local business associations in Stockton, California, provides free home security checks by law enforcement officials and public education programs on the adequacy of building codes, security standards for new structures, and the need for legislative controls on locksmithing and key duplicating.

A similar program (labelled "Operation Identification") undertaken by the Monterrey Park, California, Police Department involves etching driver's license numbers on items of value in order both to speed their recovery in the event of theft and—more primarily—to discourage theft in the first place by impeding the fencing operation.[9] Although initial reports on both these programs are favorable and both have been implemented elsewhere in the United States, available information is still insufficient to permit evaluation of their long-term efficacy.

In addition to programs operated by the regular police, a number of private and volunteer forces offer security services to communities. Although most privately owned security organizations seem to service the nonresidential market,[10] a variety of citizen groups have organized for the surveillance and protection of their own communities. Opinion seems divided on the value of their efforts. Although James Q. Wilson has described citizen auxiliaries as perhaps "the single most effective addition to police practice" and has urged the President of the United States to use his office to enlist citizen interest in such programs,[11] others have reached opposite conclusions. Smith, for example, observed:

> Experience has shown that it is not alone the super defenders of hearth and home who clamor for an opportunity to serve. Truculent, disorderly, intolerant, and downright vicious elements also flock to police standards . . . for motives of their own, and with objectives foreign to the maintenance of civil peace.[12]

In fact, citizen defense organizations frequently do encounter suspicion or hostility from regular police and from the community they seek to serve. Since they are not institutionally established in the same way as regular police, they face severe problems in obtaining resources and maintaining organizational integrity. Also, lacking the legal authority to perform such police operations as arrest or search and seizure, they are generally confined to the role of observers. Finally, since the nature of "observers' " work is frequently boring, the attrition rate among members is high. After three and one half years of "observation," the founder of one housing authority patrol reported that he had not seen anything "really suspicious" and saw the work as "mostly tedious duty."[13] Several other participants have reported that their patrols appeared to have more effect on morale than on actual crime incidence. However, visible guards patrolling on foot in limited areas such as an old people's home or a playground have been reported in some instances to reduce vandalism and physical assaults.[14]

In summary, available studies suggest that the effect of citizen patrols on the incidence of residential crime is problematic. The most effective crime prevention activity appears to be the use of police supplementary organizations for observation of specific premises, e.g., unarmed guards at building entrances in housing project areas. Attempts by citizen patrols to duplicate regular police activities by engaging in general patrol and investigative activities seem to be no more effective than regular police, in many cases less so, and certainly much riskier; but they may, nevertheless, prove valuable, if only for purposes of morale.

Since none of the areas surveyed for the present study had developed citizen patrol groups, no additional information could be gathered regarding this form of protection. However, the household survey did pose several questions aimed at citizens' views on crime prevention and involvement in preventive activities, and the results were rather discouraging for advocates of the community approach to crime control. Table 5-4 indicates almost one-third of the respondents had no clear idea about how to go about reducing crime, and among those who did have at least one specific idea (51 percent), little agreement could be reached. (No more than 11 percent of the responses mentioned the same solution.)

Table 5-4. What, if Anything, Would You Like to See Done in Your Neighborhood to Reduce Crime?*

	Victims	Nonvictims	Total
More police patrol	10%	11%	11%
More foot patrol	9	9	9
Better street lighting	11	6	8
Deal with drug problem	15	5	6
Police protection unspecified	7	5	6
More police (numbers)	8	5	5
Police-community relations	13	10	10
Recreation or discipline for teenagers	4	4	4
Other physical security	11	4	5
Deal with social problems (jobs, etc.)	5	2	3
Don't know	20	31	29
No crime in neighborhood	1	12	10

*Figures based on multiple responses.

Also, in spite of the difficulties of the police in combatting common neighborhood crimes, most people seem to view the police as the main crime prevention agents. Forty-one percent of the respondents suggested something to do with the police—more patrols, more foot patrols, more policemen, better police-community relations, etc. Another 13 percent thought crime could be reduced by improved physical security of the neighborhood—particularly the street lighting. Only six percent of the respondents suggested that dealing with the drug problem might lessen crime. Finally, victims were somewhat more likely to have ideas about crime reduction than were nonvictims. (Twenty percent of the victims said they "didn't know" how to reduce crime, compared to 31 percent of the nonvictims.)

In view of the confusion and lack of agreement evidenced by Table 5-4, the low level of neighborhood involvement in crime preventive activities did not seem surprising. Only one out of five persons interviewed had even met with neighbors or other groups to *talk* about crime in the neighborhood and only seven percent—mostly victims—had decided to do anything about it. Most of these (few) people became active in a neighborhood group with a multiproblem orientation rather than in a specifically crime oriented group. When asked whether they had heard of private citizens' neighborhood patrol groups, 57 percent of the sample indicated familiarity with this idea, and 65 percent indicated approval. More victims (77 percent) thought it was a "good idea" than nonvictims (63 percent), who were somewhat less familiar with the idea and unsure of its effect. Generally, however, people seemed to be favorably disposed toward neighborhood patrol groups.

However, despite the fact that the majority were familiar with and positive about neighborhood patrol groups, no one recommended them as a way to reduce crime in the neighborhood (although the questions about such groups were asked prior to the requests for recommendations), and only very few had even gotten together with their neighbors in any kind of group where crime was an issue.

The responses to all these questions indicated that the survey sample, for the most part, viewed neighborhood crime problems as outside their own control or the control of their neighbors—and to some extent, they may be right. Most of the social and behavioral characteristics correlated in this report with high residential crime rates are not readily amenable to change by citizen action groups. People cannot easily alter their occupancy patterns, income level, or the degree to which they and their neighbors feel "cohesive," but they do have some control over their own fear levels—and it seems probable that a lowering of the fear level might result in some constructive action.

This is not to suggest that all fears are unjustified, but only that accurate information on the nature and extent of residential crimes would permit people to make more rational calculations about their own victimization probabilities. Were people aware, for example, that burglary—by far the most common residential crime—is normally nonviolent, that the probability of victimization through residential robbery in most areas is generally remote, and that stranger-to-stranger murder or rape on residential premises is extremely uncommon, they might conclude that such common-sense measures as theft insurance and better doors and locks would be the cheapest and best protection of their homes against the threat of residential crime. (Less than 20 percent of the survey sample had such insurance and, as noted in Chapter 4, only 8 percent had standard door protection.) In sum, well-informed citizens might not only "sleep better at night," but also provide more adequately for the security of their homes and work more imaginatively with their neighbors to safeguard their common territory.

ENVIRONMENT

As discussed in Chapter 3, control of crime through modification of the physical environment has received considerable attention in recent years—partly through the publication of two popular books on the subject: Newman's *Defensible Space* and Jacob's *Death and Life of the Great American Cities.* Also, as noted in Chapter 3, the present study was unable to confirm any clear correlation between the physical layout of an area and its residential burglary rate (although the lack of such correlation was by no means definitively determined either). RA 83, the North End, a mixed land use area with many people regularly on the street, did evidence a very low burglary rate, but other areas of similar characteristics (622, Kenmore Square; 145, Copley/Prudential) displayed extremely high rates. Also, as noted in Chapter 4, the size of buildings did not appear closely correlated with their victimization probabilities. In one housing project area (RA 256), the larger (seven-story) buildings did appear to be victimized more consistently than the smaller (three-story) buildings, but, in general, small multiunit structures were, in fact, victimized more often than large—although the data presented in Chapter 3 had indicated that *areas* with a concentration of large multiunit structures were victimized more often than other areas.

Only in areas of exceptional access security (i.e., luxury high-rise apartments protected by guards and surveillance devices) did characteristics of the physical environment seem to have a conspicuous and consistent impact on the residential crime rate. However, the degree to which this kind of "access security" might be extended to the larger community is limited by both the size of the area to be secured and its population characteristics. A few large, multiunit structures in a concentrated land area can be fairly readily secured by guards, alarms, etc., but a number of smaller structures, spread over a larger area, cannot achieve the same security without enormous—and socially unacceptable—costs. Also, middle-class working people, or senior citizens, for example, would be much more likely to adapt to and enforce the security control than would, say, low income youngsters in a housing project. Finally, the social desirability of such "access-secure" housing—even if obtainable on any community-wide scale—seems extremely doubtful: the prospect of whole communities converted into armed fortresses is not an appealing one.

Clearly, more research needs to be done on the interaction of urban design with the crime experience of an area. Much of what has been done is either impressionistic in nature, or focused on areas so small and/or idiosyncratic as to limit the applicability of the observations to the larger community. Probably the most fruitful directions for future research would lie in some kind of objectification of design characteristics, which would permit a consistent comparison of crime rates among areas of measured comparability of design. Ultimately, it seems that such research would most productively aim at an optimal blending of various approaches to design, so as to insure maximum respect for the lifestyles and behavior patterns of individual residents and maximum adaptability to existing land use characteristics.

As regards the steps that an individual citizen might take to alter his own environment and thereby increase his own protection, some conflict in opinion emerged among burglars interviewed for the study. The recommendations of the burglars, presented in Table 5-5, also show some interesting inconsistencies with other information obtained from interviews.

Table 5–5.   What Precautions Would the Interviewees Advise?

	Total	Age			Race		Drug Use	
		Under 18	18-25	Over 25	W	Non W	DU	Non DU
Burglar alarms	20%	14%	17%	30%	26%	12%	18%	21%
Strong locks[a]	45	62	42	35	40	50	41	48
Strong doors & frames	7	14	6	0	6	7	2	8
Dog	20	24	21	13	18	21	18	21
Window locks or bars	18	29	17	13	16	21	18	19
Full time occupant	20	29	19	13	10	31	20	19
Lights on	14	5	17	17	24	2	14	15
Rapid playing[b]	7	0	8	9	10	2	9	4
Other	34	24	33	52	40	31	41	31
Total answering	92	21	48	23	50	42	44	48

Examples

[a]Six people specifically recommended the New York type police lock.

[b]Notify and know neighbors (4)—electrify windows (3) have screens on windows (3)—don't have any expensive things (3)—have plexiglass windows (2)—have an insurance policy (3)—have a gun (2)—leave the door open (2).

As is apparent from Table 5-5, strong locks were advocated most often by the interviewees, yet when they were asked whether strong locks would deter them personally from entering, only 5 percent indicated that the locks would deter, 33 percent that they might, and 63 percent that the locks would have no effect. (See Appendix E, Table E-1, for a more detailed summary of interviewees' evaluations of deterrents.) Personal bravado, of course, may have prejudiced their responses, and the skill tests conducted in conjunction with the interviews suggest that this may in fact be the case. Very few of the interviewees demonstrated much sophistication in their approach to the various doors and locks constructed for this study. Also, the data presented in Chapter 4 on portal security indicated that standard locks (dead latch, dead bolt, vertical bolt) installed on standard doors did have a deterrent effect, although the sample size was too small to permit definitive conclusions.

In any case, since police records indicate that 21 percent of a sample of reported burglaries are made through unlocked doors and windows, it would seem that, at the very least, residents could remember to lock their doors and windows on leaving. Innercity apartment dwellers might also find the installation of secure locks on their one or two doors leading to their unit to be a relatively inexpensive and effective precaution against the unskilled burglars most prominent in their neighborhoods. Suburban home-owners, however, who have many more portals to secure against more highly skilled offenders, would probably find this approach not cost-effective and would be better off simply purchasing insurance.

Another popular recommendation, the burglar alarm, did receive a relatively good deterrent rating: as indicated in Table 5-5, 20 percent of the interviewees recommended the alarm as a precaution, while 36 percent indicated that the evidence of an alarm would definitely deter them. (See Appendix E, Table E-1.) Since alarms were recommended most often by the over-25 age group, and since these devices are quite expensive to install, they are probably most cost-effective for the wealthy suburban resident, who generally has to contend with the older burglars and who may have items of substantial value to protect. Dogs were also recommended by 20 percent of the interviewees, and 22 percent indicated that the presence of a dog would definitely deter them. Needless to say, however, the ownership of a dog is not a practical choice for many people since urban apartments frequently have no dog policies, and since those poeple who want to live with a dog and can support one generally own one anyway.

Finally, few of the interviewees were enthusiastic about other commonly mentioned burglary deterrents: only 9 percent noted good lighting, and 5 percent, "strong doors," as salient deterrents, and although actual occupancy appeared to be the most effective deterrent (both on the admission of the interviewees and other data collected for this study), few interviewees felt that they could be deceived by simulated occupancy (i.e., radios playing, lights left on).

Although arrested burglars are not the only (and by no means, the most disinterested) judges of the effectiveness of protective measures against burglary, they did provide the only "quantifiable" evaluation of these measures that could be obtained within the limits of the present study. That is, since very few of the households surveyed for this study possessed standard doors and locks, burglar alarms, window bars or dogs, no more objective assessment could be made of the effectiveness of these protective measures. The subject of household protective measures, then, also seems ripe for future research of a quantitative sort—particularly in view of the amount of attention this subject has received in the popular press of late. Individual citizens, confused by the conflicting advice of former burglars, law enforcement officials, locksmiths and journalists, would undoubtedly profit from an objective cost-benefit analysis of security options available to them.

SUMMARY

This study has examined the three components of the residential crime problem—the offender, his victim, and his environment—and evaluated the possibilities for controlling this problem by means of the criminal justice system, community action, and environmental alterations. From this evaluation, four rough models emerge for the control of residential crime.

1. The criminal justice model, whereby police patrol and investigation are used to deter, detect, and apprehend offenders while the court and correctional agencies punish and or rehabilitate them. The present research as well as other studies have cast doubt upon the efficacy of this model for various reasons, but nevertheless, this appears to be the one most relied upon by citizens.
2. The social control or urban village model, whereby neighborhood residents manifest a strong territorial concern which acts as a deterrent to potential offenders. In central cities, such neighborhoods are usually tightly knit ethnic areas, constituting, in effect, urban villages. Regardless of location they displayed low victimization rates.
3. The limited access or fortress model (typically comprised of luxury apartment complexes) whereby physical arrangements (gates, guards, closed circuit television) limit access to residents or persons who can pass a security check. Like the urban village, this is an atypical form of enclave living by a homogenous group—in this instance, upper income persons. This model also displayed low rates regardless of location.
4. The distance model whereby persons locate their residences sufficiently far away from the urban core problem areas. This model, too, displayed low rates unless it was comparatively affluent.

Given the ineffectiveness of the first model, and for most people, the unavailability or undesirability of the other three, future research might be best directed toward developing a model which would blend the deterrent effects of the criminal justice system with citizens' anticrime efforts and improved environmental design in the most effective way. It is possible, for example, that the "rapid response" technique of the police could become a more meaningful deterrent to residential crime if environmental characteristics could be modified to maximize surveillance possibilities and encourage a sense of territorial concern among residents; citizens would take a few more precautions aimed at "slowing down" the prospective burglar so that his suspicious activities might attract the attention of neighbors; and observing neighbors might feel a "social commitment" sufficient to prompt them to summon the police. None of these steps would require massive changes in the existing scheme of things, yet, acting in concert, they might form the basis of an effective model for the control of residential crime.

As our present study has implied, however, the effectiveness of any model or strategy will depend most critically on its ability to account for the specific characteristics of burglars, victims, and locales. An effective strategy against juvenile burglars working in inner-city housing projects may be ineffective against older burglars in low density suburban areas. A strategy to secure one area may displace burglars into another, thus simply transferring the risk to a different segment of the population. Most undesirably of all, a strategy to combat burglary may increase robbery.

Displacement, whether geographic or functional, in fact looms as one of the major obstacles to any strategy for the control of residential crime. Unfortunately, however, since the concerted programs for crime reduction are for the most part only of recent origin, very little information exists regarding the differential side-effects of various strategies. One Rand study[15] did analyze the effects of police "saturation" (substantial increases in manpower to heighten the suggestion of omnipresence) in a Manhattan precinct and noted an apparent displacement of visible crimes[e] to areas immediately adjacent to the experimental precinct. The study found no evidence of a functional displacement within the experimental area—that is, robbers did not appear to switch to burglary. Another study indicated that intensive police patrol during the evening hours produced a reduction in certain types of crime but an increase in the number of these crimes committed in the late afternoon.[16] The widespread installation of burglar alarms in commercial establishments in an Iowa city reportedly was effective in curtailing commercial burglary but led to an increase in residential burglaries.[17] These three instances of crime displacement by area, time, and type of target illustrate some of the dimensions of the displacement problem.

---

[e]The study also noted that 'saturation' seemed to have no effect on the less visible crimes.

However, until more complete information does become available, assessment of the displacement potential of any strategy against residential burglary will have to depend on analysis of the variable factors governing the present distribution of residential burglary rates. As the foregoing analysis implies, the displacement effects of a strategy will be limited by the characteristics of the burglar against whom it is directed, and the characteristics of the environment in which it is implemented. If, for example, the present target choice of a young, black "housing project burglar" were foreclosed, he could not readily switch his focus of operations to white suburbs, where he would find himself conspicuous, would lack information about the targets, and would probably feel unwilling to spend the time required to plan a hit and transport himself to and from the target. He would, however, be quite likely to continue his operations in vulnerable areas adjacent to his own project. Likewise, the older white burglar, accustomed to working in relatively affluent apartments, would find it difficult to operate in the inner-city ghetto, where he too would feel conspicuous and would probably be unwilling to operate with the frequency necessary to maintain his accustomed level of income. A move to the suburbs, however, might be accomplished with ease.

Obviously, these two examples are very simplified, but they do indicate how an understanding of burglar behavior and environmental factors may be applied to the prediction of displacement patterns. Since these patterns will ultimately determine the success and acceptibility of any crime control program, they are deserving of much more attention than they have hitherto received. Although our study of the Boston area simply sought to analyze the present rates and patterns of residential crime, without specific regard to problems of displacement, the findings of the study may also serve to indicate fruitful directions for future research in this area.

NOTES

1.   A. Ganz and T. Freeman, *Population and Income of the City of Boston* (Boston: Redevelopment Authority Research Dept., 1972): 36.

2.   J.Q. Wilson, M. Moore, and D. Wheat, "The Problem of Heroin," *The Public Interest* 29 (1972): 6-7.

3.   Samuel G. Chapman, *Police Patrol Readings* (Springfield: Thomas, 1958): 77; O.W. Wilson and Roy C. McLaren, *Police Administration,* 3rd edition (New York: McGraw Hill, 1972); George D. Eastman, ed., *Municipal Police Administration* (Washington, D.C.: ICMA, 1972): 77-78; and Raymond Clift, *A Guide to Modern Police Thinking* (Cincinnati: W. Anderson Company, 1956): 20.

4.   Leonard H. Goodman, Trudy Miller, and Paul DeForrest, *A Study of the Deterrent Value of Crime Prevention Measures as Perceived by Criminal Offenders* (Washington, D.C.: Bureau of Social Research, 1966).

5.   See John Conklin, *Robbery and the Criminal Justice System* (Philadelphia: J.B. Lippincott Co., 1972): 134.

6.   Peter W. Greenwood, *An Analysis of the Apprehension Activities of the New York City Police Department* (New York: Rand Institute, 1970).

7.   Op. cit., Goodman et al. : 47.

8.   See, for example, Orin Church, "Crime Prevention—A Stitch in Time," *The Police Chief* (March 1970): 52-54.

9.   Above cited in *Standards for Burglary Prevention* (McLean, Virginia: Research Analysis Corporation, September 1971).

10.   James S. Kaklik and Sorrel Wildhorn, *Private Police in the United States* (Washington, D.C.: Department of Justice, 1972).

11.   James Q. Wilson, "Crime and Law Enforcement," *Agenda for the Nation,* Kermit Gordon, ed. (Washington, D.C.: Brookings Institute): 186, 206.

12.   Bruce Smith, *Police Systems in the United States* (New York: Harper, 1960): 314.

13.   Gary T. Marx and Dane Archer, "Picking Up the Gun: Some Organizational and Survey Data on Community Police Patrols," (M.I.T.-Harvard Joint Center for Urban Studies Typescript, 1972).

14.   Ibid.: 19.

15.   S. James Press, *Some Effects of an Increase in Police Manpower in the 20th Precinct in New York City* (New York: Rand Institute, 1971).

16.   Mentioned in Michael D. Maltz, *Evaluation of Crime Control Programs* (Washington, D.C.: U.S. Government Printing Office, 1972): 21.

17.   Ibid.: 35.

Appendixes

APPENDIX A(1): OTHER RESIDENTIAL CRIMES

In conjunction with the present study, statistics on various types of offenses in the Boston area were analyzed to determine what proportion of each type of offense could be classed as residential in nature. As anticipated by the discussion in the text, only the crimes of robbery and burglary occurred between strangers on residential premises with sufficient frequency to merit further analysis as "residential" crimes. Other crimes were analyzed as follows:

Rape

Of the 92 rapes (12 percent of the city total) which were reported to the police in the 39 Boston areas studied, only six took place between strangers in a residence.

Murder

28 murders (9 percent of the city total) were reported in the 39 studied areas, of which three were possibly residential in nature. However, because of the small sample size and the gravity of the offense, a further analysis was made of all 321 murders which occurred in Boston during the years 1969-1971. Seven were clearly perpetrated by strangers on residential premises, five in connection with a robbery, and two with an apparent burglary. In an additional twelve cases (comprising 13 victims) the victim was found dead on residential premises, but the perpetrator and motives were not identified. In some instances, the victim was thought to have been in a quarrel just prior to the murder; in others, the victim was apparently a prostitute or drug pusher, so that the crime may have arisen out of "professional" disputes. Some of the unidentified cases occurring inside the dwelling clearly involved unlawful entry, but even this fact does not guarantee that the perpetrator was a stranger. In any event, the probability of being murdered by a stranger in a home appears remote (on the order of one in 100,000 annually for the average Bostonian).

Arson

Arson against a residence is usually of a minor nature involving the burning of a part of the dwelling such as a porch. Only three respondents in the household survey reported sustaining an arson against residential premises, which would result in an annual rate of approximately 3/1,000 households.

Vandalism

Although most acts of vandalism are minor in nature, it does appear a relatively common crime.[a] A 1969 survey of a random sample of Boston house-

---

[a]The largest part of the national dollar loss to vandalism is incurred by public buildings and facilities. See Stephen Cutler and Albert J. Reiss, Jr., "Crimes Against Public

holds (N = 500) reported an annual vandalism rate of 62/1,000.[b] The household
survey conducted for this study reported a rate of 80/1,000 households, and
an extensive study of a Boston housing project found a vandalism rate of
1,844/1,000.[c] Thus, although a minor crime, the frequency of occurrence
in certain areas, such as housing projects, may constitute a serious problem.

and Quasi-Public Organizations in Boston, Chicago, and Washington, D.C." (A special
survey for the President's Commission on Law Enforcement and Administration of Justice,
1966), cited in *Task Force Report: Crime and Its Impact—An Assessment* (Washington:
U.S. Government Printing Office, 1967): 46.

[b]See Floyd Fowler, *How the People See Their City: Boston 1969* (Cambridge: Joint Center for Urban Studies of MIT and Harvard, 1970): 115.

[c]Deborah Blumin, *Victims: A Study of Crime in a Boston Housing Project* (Boston: Mayor's Office of Justice Administration, 1973).

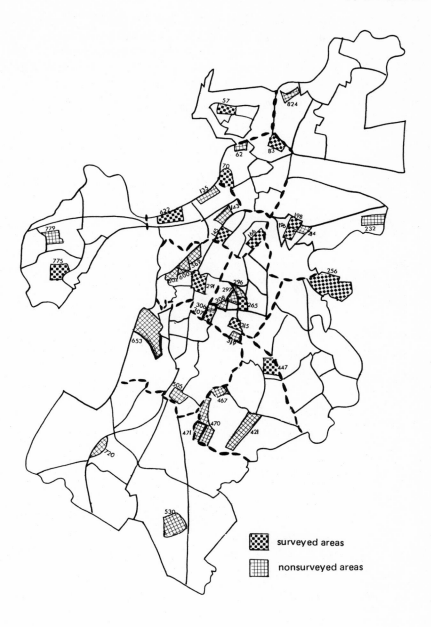

Figure A(2)-1. Selected Police Reporting Areas: City of Boston

Broken lines—Police Districts
Solid lines—Neighborhoods

Figure A(2)-2.   Neighborhoods Within Boston Police Districts

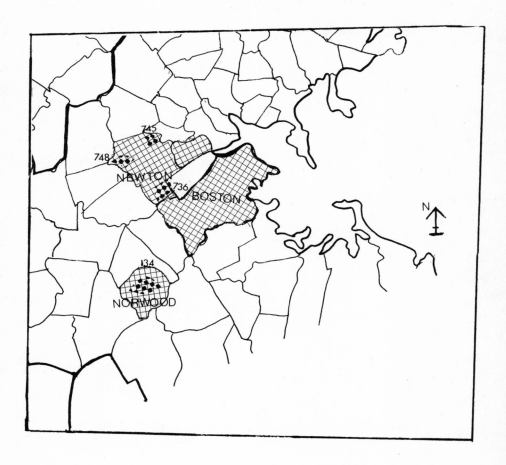

Figure A(2)-3. Suburban Reporting Areas

APPENDIX A(3): TABLES

Table A(3)-1.   Location of Reporting Areas by Police District and Neighborhood—City of Boston

Police District	Reporting Area	Neighborhood
1	62	West End
	70*	Beacon Hill
	83*	North End
3	421	Mattapan
	447*	Mt. Bowdoin
	467	Mattapan
	470-71	Mattapan
4	135	Beacon Commonwealth
	622*	Kenmore Sq.-B.U.
	143	Prudential-Copley Sq.
	145*	Prudential-Copley Sq.
	166*	South Bay-City Hosp.
		Castle Sq.-South End
5	530	Hyde Park-Readville
	720	West Roxbury
6	196*-98	Broadway
	214	Broadway
	232	Telegraph Hill-Beach Front
7	824	Maverick-Central Sq.
9	265*	Sav Mor
	296	Sav Mor
	297	Washington Park
	306	Grove Hall West
	307*	Grove Hall West
	308	Washington Park
	315*	Grove Hall West
	319	Grove Hall West
10	291*	Jackson Square
	589	Mission Hill Housing Proj.
	600	Mission Hill Housing Proj.
	602	Mission Hiss Proper
11	256*	Columbia Point
13	505*	Forest Hill
	653	Moss Hill Sect.
14	775*	Chestnut Hill-Aberdeen
	779	Brighton Center
15	57*	City Square

*Household survey area.

Table A(3)-2. Location of Reporting Areas by Suburban Town and Neighborhood

City	Reporting Area	Neighborhood
Newton	736*	Chestnut Hill
	745*-48	Newtonville-Auburndale
Norwood	134*	Central Norwood-Willet Pond

APPENDIX B(1): INTERVIEW PROCEDURE

Interviewees

Interviewees were sought among probationers at an inner city and an outlying district court, and among prisoners at two houses of correction which serve the city of Boston and a large portion of its suburban area, respectively. District court probation departments and houses of correction supervise the vast majority of persons convicted of various burglary-related offenses (see Chapter 5, Table 5-2). There was no attempt to interview nonadjudicated persons suspected of being burglars, since (1) authorities generally are not permitted to furnish such information and (2) it would not be in the suspect's interest to speak frankly about any burglaries that he committed but was not convicted for.

To control for individual veracity, each interviewee was given a skill test in which he demonstrated his methods of attack on actual doors, locks, and windows which were specially constructed for the project. His criminal history was also checked against his own statements. Based on these controls and the personal observations of the interviewers, most interviewees seemed candid, and their answers generally fit well with data collected in separate components of the study, such as the police records analysis and the household victimization study. Nevertheless, despite the above controls and the staff assessment of the results, the offender interview section should be seen as primarily exploratory in nature. Even though findings are presented in quantitative as well as narrative form, sample size and method of selection prohibit blanket application of the findings to the general burglar population. However, it is hoped that this study will be useful not only for its data, but as a guide to similar studies of a more ambitious nature. To aid such efforts, the sections below on interviewing methods have been developed more extensively than would be necessary for this project alone.

Interview Techniques

Preparations for the interviews included:

1. Collection of slides of different housing types—actual housing photographed

was in other Northeastern cities which had housing stock similar to the Boston area. Local housing was not used because, as anticipated, the interviewees were most curious about the exact location of the residences shown.

2. Design of interview questionnaire, score sheet, and skill test.
3. Selection and training of interviewers.
4. Pretest of interviews.
5. Adjustments of interview methods, questionnaire, score sheet, and skill test.

The pretests were given both to nonoffenders with knowledge or residential burglary (including a police detective, a criminologist, and a security specialist), and to inmates at a local house of correction. These pretests enabled the following assessments to be made before the final interviews began:

1. The slides worked well both in interesting interviewees initially and in eliciting specific and useful information.
2. More information was obtained in less structured interviews; that is, when interviewers asked several broad questions with follow-up questions rather than adhering strictly to a question and answer format.
3. The interviews would be taped. Interviewers obtained more information when they could concentrate on the conversation and not write down all the responses. Moreover, contrary to expectations, none of the interviewees objected to a tape recorder being used, provided that confidentiality and anonymity were assured.
4. Each interviewer would score his own interview as soon as possible afterwards. Experiments with a second person scoring the replies during the interview were unsatisfactory, both because key comments were missed and because the unstructured format made it difficult to keep track on the score sheet.
5. Although slides were effective in helping to pinpoint the interviewees' usual area of operation, they were not helpful in pinpointing access and detection variables important to the interviewee. These slides were therefore eliminated and the information obtained through direct questions.
6. Locks and doors used in the skill test were destroyed so frequently (five during the pretests) that interviewees would be asked to demonstrate their skills only up to the point where significant force was used.
7. The interviewees were so cooperative that more probing questions were added to the regular interviews: questions referring, for example, to previous illegal activities, disposal of the goods, and to use of drugs.
8. Because of the detailed and extensive information obtained from the interviews, computer runoffs would have to be made for a satisfactory analysis to be accomplished.

Selection and Training of Interviewers

All interviewers had some background in fields related to the subject matter of the interview. One, for example, was a doctoral candidate in sociology, specializing in crime and delinquency; another was a third year law student. One interviewer had worked with delinquents and minority action groups. Interviewers were both male and female and were ethnically mixed. In general there were no major differences in the reaction of various subjects to different interviewers.

Interviewers were given interview and scoring instructions. The pretest interviewers watched at least the first interview given by each person to see that the results were satisfactory. Since interviewers scored their own interviews as soon as possible after they were undertaken, when the hundredth interview was completed, all the interviews except the last few had been scored. Hand tallies were made periodically to indicate the initial direction of the findings.

The average interview lasted about one and a half to two hours and consisted of the slide test and the skill test. The latter took an average of 20 minutes. Interviewers worked in two-person teams. In general they found it unproductive to do more than four interviews per day. The average interviewer completed about 13 interviews during the course of the project.

After 100 interviews were completed and scored, the score sheets were handchecked for errors. At this point three interviews were discarded for technical reasons—e.g., indistinct recording so that an insufficient number of responses could be heard.

APPENDIX B(2): TABLES

Note: The percentage in the following tables do not add up to 100 percent in some cases because questions permitted multiple responses or interviewees failed to respond.

Table B(2)-1. Education Levels of Interviewees, in Total and by Age, Race, and Drug Use

			Age		*Race*		*Drug Use*	
	Total	*Under 18*	*18-25*	*Over 25*	*W*	*Non W*	*DU*	*Non DU*
Under 8th	9%	29%	4%	4%	13%	4%	2%	16%
Ed. level 8-9th	12	33	8	4	13	11	13	12
10-11th	42	33	53	28	34	51	46	39
12th	21	0	22	36	25	16	27	14
Over 12th	15	5	14	28	13	18	13	18
Total	97	21	51	25	52	45	48	49
Median ed.	11th	10th	11th	11th	10th	11th	11th	10th

Table B(2)-2.   Type of Occupations Interviewees Had Held, in Total and by Age, Race, and Drug Use

		Age			Race		Drug Use	
	Total	Under 18	18-25	Over 25	W	Non W	DU	Non DU
Unskilled	53%	71%	49%	40%	59%	44%	52%	53%
Semiskilled	61	14	74	72	65	56	67	55
Armed services	8	0	12	8	14	2	10	6
Skilled, managerial, or professional	8	0	6	20	8	9	8	8
Never been employed	7	24	4	0	6	9	6	8
Total	97	21	51	25	52	45	48	49

Occupational Level (row group label)

Table B(2)-3.   What Was the Most Interviewees Had Ever Earned in a Week

		Age			Race		Drug Use	
	Total	Under 18	18-25	Over 25	W	Non W	DU	Non DU
Less than $50	10%	36%	4%	0%	5%	15%	5%	16%
$50-100	24	47	28	0	34	15	26	23
$100-200	43	12	47	57	39	46	49	36
Over $200	23	0	21	43	22	24	21	25
Total	87	17	47	23	41	46	43	44

Table B(2)-4.   What Other Illegal Activities Did Interviewees Say They Had Engaged in, in Total, and by Age, Race, and Drug Use?

		Age			Race		Drug Use	
	Total	Under 18	18-25	Over 25	W	Non W	DU	Non DU
Pursesnatching	10%	21%	8%	4%	9%	11%	11%	9%
Robbery	21	5	33	8	26	16	26	16
Autotheft	50	47	54	42	55	43	45	55
Assault	29	21	25	25	26	23	23	25
Possessing narcotics	56	47	71	33	57	52	100	18
Selling narcotics	14	5	15	21	15	14	23	13
Other*	25	16	29	25	23	27	38	11
None	17	21	8	29	15	18	6	27
Total	91	19	48	24	47	44	47	44

Other Admitted Illegal Activities (row group label)

Examples:
*Stealing checks, forgery, pickpocketing, con man, shoplifting, pimping, arson, smuggling, stealing from tills, receiving stolen goods.

Table B(2)-5. What Other Nonresidential Buildings, if Any, Had Interviewees Worked on?

Nonresidential		*Total*	*Age*			*Race*		*Drug Use*	
			Under 18	*18-25*	*Over 25*	*W*	*Non W*	*DU*	*Non DU*
	Stores	63%	70%	64%	52%	65%	60%	66%	59%
	Offices	32	11	33	52	39	24	35	29
	Restaurants	9	5	7	17	6	12	7	10
	Factories	6	5	4	11	11	0	5	8
	Others	27	35	28	11	27	24	28	24
	Total	76	17	42	17	43	33	39	37

Table B(2)-6. What Housing Types Were Interviewees Least Likely to Operate in, Overall and by Age, Race, and Drug Use?

	Total	*Age*			*Race*		*Drug Use*	
		Under 18	*18-25*	*Over 25*	*W*	*Non W*	*DU*	*Non DU*
Housing projects	40%	23%	38%	53%	46%	30%	42%	34%
Luxury apartments	25	28	28	16	22	29	21	29
Single family houses	21	28	22	12	10	34	22	18
Row houses	6	9	6	4	10	2	6	6
Multifamily houses	5	9	4	4	2	4	4	6
Old brick apartments	3	0	2	8	10	0	2	4
Total	97	21	51	25	52	45	48	49

Table B(2)-7.   What Were the Main Reasons Interviewees Gave for Their Choices by Age, Race, and Drug Use?

	Total	Age			Race		Drug Use	
		Under 18	*18-25*	*Over 25*	*W*	*Non W*	*DU*	*Non DU*
Too many people around[a]	35%	33%	41%	28%	38%	31%	35%	35%
Not profitable	31	10	35	48	36	24	29	33
Police/security patrols	31	57	29	16	27	36	23	39
Neighbors surveillance[b]	21	33	14	24	17	24	17	24
Feels conspicuous[c]	20	24	22	12	11	29	19	20
Total	97	21	51	25	52	45	48	49

Examples

[a]People walking by in the street or in the apartment building; children playing outside.

[b]Neighbors likely to be watching from inside (the next door house or apartment) "Too many nosy neighbors . . ., Always watching out for strangers, "Couldn't get to the front door before the neighbor would call the cops."

[c]Out of place in the neighborhood—race or age different from residents.

Table B(2)-8.   Characteristics of Arrested Burglars, Selected Areas, 1970-1971

Type of Area	Age			Race	
	Under 17	*17-24*	*Over 25*	*W*	*NW*
Large public housing project (N = 78)	30%	70%	0%	NA	NA
Inner city apt. area, predominantly white transient (N = 162)	14	56	30	59%	50%
Predominantly black inner city (N = 518)	34	50	16	16	84
Predominantly white suburban (N = 125)	23	59	18	93	7

Source: Police records analysis.

Table B(2)-9. What Type of Information Would Interviewees Want?

Type of Information	*Total*	*Age*			*Race*		*Drug Use*	
		Under 18	*18-25*	*Over 25*	*W*	*Non W*	*DU*	*Non DU*
Occupancy of residents	70%	76%	63%	80%	65%	76%	58%	82%
Valuables available	34	43	27	36	29	40	27	41
Burglar alarm	36	34	36	36	29	47	35	39
Police or security patrols	14	0	10	36	17	11	13	16
Location of entrances	15	19	12	24	17	13	13	18
Escape routes	20	19	16	28	17	22	15	24
Total	97	21	51	25	52	45	48	49

Table B(2)-10. How Did Those Interviewees Who Wanted to Know the Occupancy Pattern of Residents and What Valuables Were Available Obtain Their Information, in Total, and by Age, Race, and Drug Use?

How Information Sought	*Total*	*Age*			*Race*		*Drug Use*	
		Under 18	*18-25*	*Over 25*	*W*	*Non W*	*DU*	*Non DU*
Res.'s Occu. Patterns								
Watches residence[a]	68%	56%	62%	85%	76%	58%	75%	63%
Asks neighbors	6	0	3	15	8	3	4	8
Signs of absence[b]	6	0	6	10	3	9	7	5
Telephones	18	12	21	15	17	18	21	15
Other[c]	24	31	31	25	23	26	29	20
Total	68	16	32	20	34	34	28	40
Valuables Available								
Window peeping	42%	55%	28%	40%	53%	33%	46%	40%
Previous entrance[d]	9	11	7	10	7	11	8	10
Tips from friends/fence	33	33	50	10	20	44	38	30
Other[e]	39	22	50	40	53	28	67	45
Total	33	9	14	10	15	18	13	20

Examples

[a]Length of time interviewees would watch residence varied from half an hour to periodically over several weeks.

[b]Newspapers outside front door, uncollected mail, old milk bottles.

[c]Asks friends; gets tip; checks newspapers; rings front door bell.

[d]May have broken in, or entered previously as a tradesman, salesman, or friend.

[e]TV aerial, air conditioner outside; sees family move in.

Table B(2)-11.   What Time of Day or Night Did Interviewees Usually Work, in Total, and by Age, Race, and Drug Use?*

	Total	Age			Race		Drug Use	
		Under 18	18-25	Over 25	W	Non W	DU	Non DU
6 am − 12 pm	41%	30%	54%	30%	29%	57%	47%	40%
12 pm − 6 pm	34	40	38	48	31	39	34	35
6 pm − 12 am	33	40	30	39	45	20	31	35
12 am − 6 am	9	10	14	0	8	11	11	8
No preferred time	5	10	4	9	8	2	6	4
Total	94	20	51	23	51	44	47	48

*As noted in the text and in Table B(2)-12, the analysis of police records generally confirmed the daytime work preferences expressed by interviewees. The only consistent deviations from the pattern of daytime attacks were found in outlying areas (RAs 134, 470, 746, and 745) and in some housing project areas (RAs 196, 256, and 600), where burglaries were more evenly distributed between day and night, The relatively high nighttime burglary rates of the housing project areas may be attributable to the fact that the youthful offenders who most often work in these areas are generally in school during the day and convene for their group activities during the evening hours. The nighttime burglary rates of the outlying areas are more difficult to explain, but may be partially influenced by the low population density of suburban neighborhoods, which makes intruders fairly conspicuous in daylight but inconspicuous after dark. Suburban residents also have more tendency to be away during the evening.

Table B(2)-12.   Time of Attack, Based on Police Records

*Month (N = 1140)**

Jan.	8.9%	May	7.3%	Sept.	6.4%		
Feb.	7.3%	June	7.9%	Oct.	8.8%	Total	
Mar.	8.8%	July	9.2%	Nov.	10.2%	99.2%	
Apr.	7.9%	Aug.	6.4%	Dec.	10.1%		

Day (N = 1666)

Mon.	16%	Fri.	16.1%		
Tues.	15.9%	Sat.	10.6%	Total	
Wed.	15.8%	Sun.	8.1%	99.5%	
Thur.	17%				

Time (N = 1632)

Day	72.4%
Night	27.5%
	99.9%

By Hours (N = 918)

0:01 A.M. − 6:00 A.M.	10.9%		
6:01 A.M. − 12:00 A.M.	16.2%	Total	
12:01 P.M. − 6:00 P.M.	47.7%	99.9%	
6:01 P.M. − 12:00 P.M.	25.1%		

*City data for 1969-1970 only because last 3 months of 1971 not available.

Table B(2)-13. What Tools and/or Weapons Did Interviewees Usually Carry, in Total and by Age, Race, and Drug Use?

		Age			Race		Drug Use	
	Total	*Under 18*	*18-25*	*Over 25*	*W*	*Non W*	*DU*	*Non DU*
Tools Wrench, vice grips	3%	0%	2%	8%	2%	4%	4%	2%
Hammer	6	10	6	4	0	13	2	10
Screwdriver	72	86	76	52	57	89	71	73
Crowbar, tire iron, jimmy	39	53	33	26	46	31	35	43
Picks, key gun	5	5	6	4	6	4	4	6
Glass cutter	7	0	14	0	8	7	13	2
Loid card	8	5	12	4	10	7	13	4
Other[a]	29	24	24	44	33	22	35	20
None	2	0	2	4	4	0	2	2
Total	97	21	51	25	52	45	48	49
Weapons Guns	8%	5%	10%	8%	13%	3%	8%	8%
Knife	7	5	7	8	8	5	11	3
Mace	5	11	5	0	5	5	5	5
Other[b]	4	5	5	0	3	5	3	5
None	75	74	74	85	73	78	70	78
Total	76	19	42	13	40	36	37	40

Examples

[a]Key, knife, lock puller.

[b]Machete, bottle.

Table B(2)-14. Location and Portal of Entry—Based on Police Records

Point of Entry (N = 1345)	
Front	61.1%
Side	6.0%
Rear	32.2%
Total	99.3%

Opening Used (N = 1584)	
Door	67.7%
Window	32.0%
Other	Less than 1%
Total	99.7%

Table B(2)-15. Which of the Methods Listed Below Did Interviewees Normally Use to Enter a Door or Window?[a]

		Total	Age			Race		Drug Use	
			Under 18	18-25	Over 25	W	Non W	DU	Non DU
Door	Prying door[c]	42%	35%	45%	42%	45%	39%	42%	42%
	Attacking lock[d]	17	26	18	4	7	26	16	18
	Direct impact[e]	11	12	14	5	17	6	14	9
	Loiding door[f]	16	8	16	25	19	14	20	13
	Picking lock[g]	6	2	4	13	5	8	3	8
	Passkey[h]	4	11	1	4	2	5	2	5
	Look for door open	4	6	2	7	5	2	3	5
	Total	90	20	46	24	49	41	46	44
Window	Breaking glass[i]	37%	41%	37%	35%	42%	32%	37%	38%
	Prying catch[j]	16	12	17	15	12	19	17	14
	Loiding catch[k]	21	23	22	17	19	24	15	26
	Cutting glass[l]	13	10	10	22	11	14	17	9
	Look for open window	13	14	14	11	15	11	14	13
	Total[b]	93	20	49	24	51	42	48	45

Method of Entry

[a]Interviewees were asked to describe what methods they would use for a typical ten entries through a door and ten entries through a window.

[b]Seven people said they only went through windows and four said they went only through doors. So they were not asked this section of the question.

Examples

[c]Using force to pry or jimmy the door and jamb apart, or to force the lock striker out of the door or wall. Usual tools—screwdriver, crowbar, or pinchbar.

[d]Breaking or taking the lock apart, thus opening the door. Usual tools—pinchbar, crowbar, screwdriver, pliers, or dent puller.

[e]Using direct physical force or ramming or attacking the door with heavy objects, thus breaking the door or taking it off its hinges. Usual tools—body (shoulder, knee, foot), crowbar, axe.

[f]Slipping thin, flexible material between door and jamb to move the bolt. Usual tools—credit card, plastic strip, screwdriver, knife.

[g]Usual tools—lock picking set, wire, file.

[h]Usual tools—skeleton key or homemade key.

[i]Smashing glass and then turning catch and opening window. Usual tools—screwdriver, rock, elbow, brick, tape.

[j]Breaking the wood between the two frames and forcing open the catch. Usual tools—screwdriver, crowbar.

[k]Placing an object between the two frames to slip open the catch. Usual tools—screwdriver, plastic strip, butterknife.

[l]Cutting glass and then turning catch and opening window. Usual tools—glasscutter, tape.

Table B(2)-16. What Was the Average Score per Hit for Interviewees, in Total, and by Age, Race, and Drug Use?

	Total	*Age*			*Race*		*Drug Use*	
		Under 18	*18-25*	*Over 25*	*W*	*Non W*	*DU*	*Non DU*
0-$50	9%	35%	2%	0	13%	4%	0	18%
$50-100	14	20	16	4	7	23	10	16
$100-300	47	40	51	44	37	58	48	47
$300-500	14	0	19	17	20	8	25	4
$500-1,000	11	5	7	22	17	3	13	9
Over $1,000	6	0	5	13	7	4	5	7
Total	86	20	43	23	46	40	40	45

Average Score per Hit

Table B(2)-17. How Many Hits per Week Did Interviewees Make, in Total and by Age, Race, and Drug Use?*

	Total	*Age*			*Race*		*Drug Use*	
		Under 18	*18-25*	*Over 25*	*W*	*Non W*	*DU*	*Non DU*
0-1	17%	25%	5%	33%	16%	17%	5%	28%
1-2	26	40	21	24	29	23	17	35
2-5	27	30	25	29	27	28	33	21
5-10	15	5	25	5	13	17	21	9
Over 10	15	0	25	10	16	15	24	7
Total	85	20	44	21	45	40	42	43

Number of Hits per Week

*These categories were used because interviewees frequently made such replies as "I do one hit every two weeks," "I make one or two hits a week," or "I do four or five hits a week."

Table B(2)-18.   What Do Interviewees Use the Money for, in Total, and by Age, Race, and Drug Use?

What Money Is Used for	Total	Age			Race		Drug Use	
		Under 18	18-25	Over 25	W	Non W	DU	Non DU
Drugs	51%	35%	67%	32%	50%	52%	98%[b]	13%[c]
Alcohol	19	15	6	48	25	11	8	29
Buys goods, clothes	55	70	47	60	48	61	42	69
Banks money	14	5	18	16	13	14	13	15
Other[a]	46	40	37	68	42	50	35	54
Total	96	20	51	25	52	44	48	48

Examples

[a]Gives to family, children; takes vacation; leads the good life—"goes to fancy restaurants"; "to live."

[b]One drug user claimed he did not buy heroin, but was given it at parties.

[c]These interviewees would buy only marijuana or hallucinogens.

Table B(2)-19.   Residential Robbery Rate per 100 Persons;[a] January 1969-December 1971

Reporting Area	Number of Incidents	Average Rate/1000 Persons
135	5	b
143	2	b
145	19	4
166	20	4
256	47	4
265	1	b
296	6	2
297	1	b
306	2	b
307	2	b
315	1	b
319	6	b
467	1	b
589	22	6
600	15	2
266	2	b

[a]Omitted areas had no robberies.

[b]Less than 1/1000.

APPENDIX C(1): CHARACTERISTICS OF RAs
DISCUSSED IN CHAPTER 3 (CRITICAL FACTORS
FOR RESIDENTIAL BURGLARY RATE)

RA 83—See Figure C(3)-5

RA 83 is located in the North End, a neighborhood of the city which is clearly defined both geographically and socially—bound on three sides by water and by an expressway on the fourth, and inhabited mainly by Italian-American families. The RA exhibits the social cohesiveness found throughout the North End: most of its largely Italian-American population are long-time residents (66 percent had resided in the area for more than five years), typically low and middle income blue-collar workers. Like that of the surrounding neighborhood, the predominant type of housing in RA 83 is the small attached multifamily structure of 5-10 units.

As is true of the North End area in general, the burglary rate of RA 83 is low, despite the fact that it exhibits almost every characteristic which would suggest a high burglary rate. It is a densely populated area in the core city, with numerous poorly-lit interior streets and alleys. Dwellings appear highly vulnerable to breaking and entering, the condition of doors and windows being extremely poor, and there are almost no special security devices in effect. However, the area maintains a high surveillance capacity: the occupancy rate is among the highest in the city, and outsiders on the streets are under constant observation by residents looking out of upper story windows or sitting outdoors. Outsiders are readily identifiable due to the stability and tightly knit ethnic quality of the community.

RA 57—See Figure C(3)-6

RA 57 is located in the City Square neighborhood of Charlestown, a district of Boston separated from the central city by water. The area exhibits a high degree of social cohesion: blue-collar Irish-American workers form the dominant group (there are no black residents); families with children predominate; the proportion of owner-occupied units is significantly higher than is generally found in the city; and the area has a low transiency rate. The surrounding City Square neighborhood is similar to RA 57, consisting mainly of small attached multifamily structures of 2-4 units and single-family townhouses.

The burglary rate for RA 57, as for the surrounding neighborhood, is low. Houses in the area do exhibit signs of physical vulnerability: front doors are generally old and loosely fitting, often with glass panes and substandard locks; many houses have cellar doors that can be pried or shoved open easily, and at least one-half have rear access through narrow alleys. The street lighting is generally standard but, because few additional street lights are present, front doorways are dark. However, several factors might account for the area's low burglary rate. Charlestown is remote from the rest of Boston: although it is connected by subway, there is little to attract outside groups—the area is not affluent, there is little night life and there is a fairly tightly knit ethnic community. What burglaries there are seem to cluster around Monument Square, where small teenage groups gather at nighttime. Since there is considerable vandalism in this area, it is possible that the same groups could be responsible for both vandalism and burglaries.

RA 505—See Figure C(3)-7

RA 505 is located in the Forest Hills neighborhood of the Jamaica Plain District. The area is an isolated one: it is neither adjacent to main thoroughfares or near a subway station; cemeteries and a large park form a barrier to other residential and commercial areas. There is a high degree of social cohesion. Residents are white, predominantly middle income white-collar workers or skilled laborers. The area has a low transiency rate, and most residents own their homes.

The burglary rate for RA 505, as for the surrounding neighborhood is low. Residences are vulnerable to breaking and entering in that, being detached single-family and small multifamily structures of 2-4 units, there are many ground level access points per unit. Doors and windows are only moderately secure due to the presence of glass panes in or near doors and the absence of special locks on doors or windows. However, these evidences of physical vulnerability seem immaterial in light of several factors which may explain the low crime rate. RA 505 is relatively isolated from and inaccessible to the core city, and there is little to attract criminal elements; the area is not conspicuously affluent. Moreover, like the surrounding neighborhood, it is a cohesive and stable area in which strangers are conspicuous.

RA 736—See Figure C(3)-8

RA 736 is in the Chestnut Hill neighborhood of Newton, a large suburb immediately west of Boston. Although it is located over five miles outside of central Boston, it is accessible by several major thoroughfares and a subway line. Residents are characteristically white, upper or middle income professionals. Couples without resident children predominate. There is a high proportion of homeowners and a concomitantly low transiency rate. RA 736 has the highest percentage of detached single-family structures of any area surveyed. Most are in sound or excellent condition and valued at $50,000 or more. The surrounding neighborhood is similar, and, like RA 736, has a medium burglary rate.

Residences in the area are vulnerable to breaking and entering because, being predominantly detached single-family houses, there are many ground-level access points per unit. Furthermore, because of large yards, fences, hedges, shrubbery, and the distance from and angle to the street of neighboring houses, many access points have poor visibility to either passersby or neighbors and are not well-lit at night. Two principal differences in crime pattern between RA 736 and most other RAs emerged: (1) one-half the breaks occurred at night, and (2) the burglars entered through windows more frequently than doors. Most entries were made forcibly through the rear or side of the building. Most breaks took place on Fridays and Saturdays and during the summer months when people were probably assumed to be away.

Several other factors increase the RAs vulnerability. The ability of a stranger to go unnoticed is further enhanced by the fact that vehicular and pedestrian traffic are light on most streets and because of the low degree of interchange between neighbors. The RAs obvious wealth makes it an attractive target, and it is easily accessible from the core city by car or by public transportation.

RA 745–See Figures C(3)-9 and 10

RA 745 consists of two noncontiguous areas of the large Boston suburb of Newton. The areas, similar in socioeconomic characteristics and housing stock, were surveyed together to determine crime patterns in suburban apartment areas. The first area, Auburndale, is approximately ten miles from central Boston, accessible by a subway line. The other, Newtonville, is about two miles nearer central Boston but not accessible by subway and difficult to locate. In both areas, residents are white, middle income white-collar workers; there are few children or elderly persons. The low degree of social cohesion is not surprising since nearly all are renters of units in new, 2-3 story multifamily garden apartments. The areas stand out from the surrounding neighborhood of single-family houses and large open spaces.

Although Auburndale and Newtonville are very similar, each being made up of garden apartments surrounded by well-tended yards, Newtonville, even though it is less accessible from the core city, has the higher burglary rate. One possible explanation may lie in the fact that, due to a very open layout with few shrubs or trees, all Auburndale apartments are highly visible, front and rear, both from other apartments and from the street. Newtonville, on the other hand, is built on a superblock pattern with many large shrubs, and entrances can only be seen from one apartment directly opposite. Another explanation might be the higher level of access security found in Auburndale: a buzzer system at entrances, glass doors reinforced with mesh at entrances and at entry to halls, and windows that cannot be pried open. In Newtonville, exterior doors have no locks, enabling strangers to enter the buildings unchallenged.

Contributing to the vulnerability of each area is the fact that RA 745 was one of the lowest areas in terms of time when dwellings were unoccupied: at least one-half the burglaries in both areas took place at the weekend when, in all cases, the residence was unoccupied.

RA 256—See Figures C(3)-11 and 12

RA 256, Columbia Point, is a large peninsula that extends into Dorchester Bay. The only housing stock in the RA, the Columbia Point housing project, is extremely isolated: the fourth side of the peninsula is bordered by expressways and railroad tracks; the project is located one-half mile out on the peninsula and is distant from any subway stop; surrounding the project are large open spaces which contrast sharply to the high concentration of structures in the project. The population is highly transient. Sixty percent are black, the rest white and Spanish-speaking. Typically, inhabitants are low income families with children, many with female heads.

The project, built in the 1950s, contains 1400 units in a mixture of 3 and 7 story buildings constructed in large superblocks. Despite the fact that Columbia Point has a security force with 3 officers on the grounds from 8:00 A.M. until midnight and a number of security devices including metal doors, and special locks on apartment doors, the burglary rate is high. The RA was the only one surveyed in which more entries were made through windows than doors, made possible even on upper floors because an offender can step across the inner corners from the ledge of the hallway window to the ledge of an apartment window. The buildings are deteriorating and there is evidence of extensive vandalism: hallways in the project are dark due to burnt-out or vandalized lights. In addition, the construction of buildings around an interior courtyard without circumventing roads prevents surveillance from police patrol cars or adequate lighting of interior corners. There is little pedestrian or vehicular traffic. Eighty-one percent of the arrested burglars in 1970 and 1971 were residents; all were under 25.

RA 622—See Figure C(3)-13

RA 622 is in the Kenmore Square-Boston University neighborhood of Boston's Back Bay district. About a mile from central Boston, it serves as a commercial nucleus, with subway and bus terminals within it and main traffic arteries criss-crossing it. Residents are typically white, young and transient, many of them students.[a] The area ranked low in social cohesion: most units are rented, and half are occupied by only one person. Large multifamily attached structures (many with 10 or more units) predominate; most are old but in sound condition. The surrounding neighborhood includes Boston University and a residential section similar to RA 622. It has a medium burglary rate.

Residences are vulnerable to burglary because of old doors and windows, because they are accessible from the rear by back streets and alleys, and because the upper floors of many buildings can be reached by fire escapes at the rear of buildings. Many apartments are located over ground floor offices,

---

[a]However, dormitories and fraternity houses were excluded from the household survey sample.

making detection less likely. In addition, RA 622 is one of the lowest in terms of time dwellings are occupied. Although the main commercial street, Commonwealth Avenue, receives a heavy flow of pedestrian and vehicular traffic day and night, and other streets are moderately trafficked, strangers easily go unnoticed in this highly transient and unstable area. Thus, although some security improvements have been made, the predominate security level is low. Burglaries occurred in every part of the area, particularly in the middle section of Bay State Road (see map). All buildings hit were multiunit, first floor units being most frequently victimized. Most entries were made through the front, usually through the door and during the day.

RA 315—See Figure C(3)-14

RA 315 is in the Grove Hall West neighborhood of Roxbury, a neighborhood that underwent urban renewal in the 1960s. It is adjacent to main thoroughfares and accessible by bus, but it is about half a mile from the nearest subway. It is inhabited by black, low income workers and some professionals. The area has a relatively low transiency rate: families with children predominate and a significant percent own their homes. Small structures of 2-4 units comprise almost all housing in the area, with the exception of a few single-family homes, one large apartment building, and several rest homes for the elderly. The surrounding neighborhood has characteristics similar to RA 315 but with a higher proportion of large multifamily structures, a street (Warren Street—see map) on which are located bars and commercial establishments, and Franklin Park, site of numerous assaults and robberies. The burglary rate for RA 315 and the neighborhood is high.

The small multifamily residences are vulnerable to breaking and entering due to the numerous ground level access points per unit. Doors with glass panes are common, and few appear to have special locks. A few special security devices were noted. (In year pervious to the study, 47 percent of the burglary victims, as opposed to 8 percent of nonvictims, have changed their security practices, presumably to try to combat the burglary rate which doubled between 1969 and 1970.) Single-family dwellings were hit more often than other types. Usually the entry was made through the front door, force commonly being used. Almost two-thirds of the burglaries took place during the day; one-half during the summer months. To an extent, the high burglary rate in the area can be explained in terms of contrasts in wealth. Although RA 315 has a low median income, some professionals (middle and high income) live in the area, particularly on Howland Street. As can be seen from the map, their houses seem the preferred targets.

APPENDIX C(2): TABLES

Table C(2)-1. 1970 Census Statistics, Surveyed Areas

Reporting area	57	70	83	145	166	196	256	265	291	307	315	447	505	622	775	736	745	134
Population	1355	2377	1349	1443	2091	3160	4708	1402	905	1029	801	791	409	3140	209	4104	251	9943
% black	---	.4%	---	38%	50%	5%	60%	86%	60%	82%	85%	83%	---	.5%	7%	2%	---	---
% under 18	30%	9%	23%	14%	41%	51%	61%	34%	24%	38%	27%	45%	30%	3%	11%	15%	9%	32%
% 62 and over	14%	18%	17%	19%	14%	10%	9%	13%	23%	5%	24%	5%	19%	.7%	51%	14%	7%	14%
Total units	459	1351	576	771	740	835	1418	483	425	376	220	250	131	510	115	647	132	3281
% in single unit structures	29%	11%	.6%	3%	6%	3%	---	11%	9%	3%	13%	7%	47%	6%	6%	78%	7%	46%
% in structures of 10 or more units	8%	38%	22%	40%	63%	72%	96%	16%	.4%	39%	.9%	---	---	42%	9%	2%	91%	22%
% owner occupied	42%	17%	12%	7%	3%	6%	---	21%	19%	6%	37%	30%	66%	8%	13%	80%	5%	52%
% renter occupied	58%	83%	88%	93%	97%	94%	100%	79%	81%	94%	63%	70%	34%	92%	87%	20%	95%	48%
% vacant	6%	7%	8%	10%	8%	4%	18%	8%	24%	6%	8%	11%	1%	10%	3%	1%	3%	4%
Value range of owner occupied structures	$12,000 $20,200	$52,300 $60,000	---	$22,500 ---	---	$6,300 $6,900	---	$11,700 $14,800	$5,400 $11,400	---	$14,400 $15,400	$13,800 ---	$21,400 $23,800	$37,700 ---	---	$51,800 ---	$29,200 ---	$28,800
Rent range	$73 $116	$167 $252	$43 $76	$88 $128	$74 $96	$53 $85	$69 $75	$91 $107	$64 $90	$99 $106	$98 $115	$83 $102	$109 $113	$132 $181	$88	$198	$222	$154
% units occupied by one-person households	21%	52%	32%	55%	31%	33%	23%	25%	35%	21%	16%	16%	10%	53%	54%	12%	29%	18%
% units occupied by female head of household	12%	2%	8%	6%	29%	32%	42%	19%	19%	33%	21%	23%	13%	2%	7%	7%	4%	7%
Family and unrelated person median income	$7,100	$7,111	$5,964	$2,650	$3,362	$3,550	$3,459	$4,909	$3,938	$5,779	$6,471	$6,694	$10,000	$1,127	$5,386	$30,482	$11,161	$12,542

--- Denotes none of this category present.

Table C(2)-2.   1970 Census Statistics, Nonsurveyed Areas

Reporting area	62	135	143	214	232	296	297	306	308	319	421	467	470-	530	589	600	602	653	720	779	824
Population	2050	2278	1174	1668	857	917	1040	1186	795	2380	1401	681	827	196	1248	2588	1416	482	531	990	1860
% black	1%	2%	1%	2%	----	86%	96%	78%	93%	96%	8%	63%	20%	----	95%	39%	8%	.7%	----	----	----
% under 18	6%	7%	3%	31%	22%	34%	49%	36%	36%	42%	20%	39%	25%	36%	59%	36%	5%	37%	25%	25%	34%
% 62 and over	13%	4%	30%	15%	28%	13%	7%	20%	13%	4%	15%	5%	15%	11%	5%	21%	13%	17%	21%	20%	12%
Total units	1386	1385	800	640	301	342	301	313	279	815	549	206	268	59	410	1038	846	126	192	305	643
% in single unit structures	----	.2%	.4%	24%	5%	11%	58%	6%	30%	3%	19%	16%	62%	53%	.4%	1%	7%	98%	26%	7%	8%
% in structures of 10 or more units	100%	57%	91%	----	23%	5%	13%	33%	----	44%	40%	6%	7%	----	87%	27%	75%	----	11%	----	.1%
% owner occupied	----	7%	----	38%	18%	26%	14%	25%	17%	12%	30%	51%	69%	42%	1%	.7%	6%	95%	48%	42%	31%
% renter occupied	100%	92%	100%	61%	81%	73%	85%	73%	82%	87%	69%	48%	30%	58%	98%	99%	93%	4%	52%	57%	67%
% vacant	11%	7%	10%	15%	4%	11%	5%	11%	5%	3%	2%	4%	1%	----	17%	14%	13%	----	2%	2%	4%
Value range of owner occupied structures	----	46,100 57,100	----	6,900 12,300	----	5,300 13,800	9,600 15,800	12,200	18,400	14,800	17,100 26,300	20,500	19,000 23,000	16,800 21,700	----	----	19,000 21,800	28,000 39,000	21,000 24,300	21,500 23,300	9,600 13,200
Rent range	$268	$158-271	$280	$46-87	$81-162	$87-102	$76-126	$76-108	$91-105	$89-126	$101-173	$118-139	$106-163	$76-88	$73	$67-183	$104-208	----	$107-141	$92-127	$64-75
% units occupied by one-person households	52%	53%	51%	25%	32%	30%	15%	21%	17%	23%	20%	10%	9%	19%	13%	40%	57%	17%	22%	15%	19%
% units occupied by female head of household	4%	3%	4%	17%	15%	17%	34%	28%	23%	31%	6%	14%	9%	5%	63%	29%	5%	11%	19%	16%	15%
Family and unrelated person median income	$6,628	$4,279	$9,421	$7,366	$8,365	$4,909	$4,962	$5,917	$5,441	$5,707	$8,903	$7,509	$8,903	$9,393	$1,139	$3,112	$6,170	$9,020	$11,161	$6,915	$7,889

---- Denotes none of this category present.

Table C(2)-3.   Residential Burglary Rate per 1000 Households,[a] Survey Areas

	1969		1970		1971[b]		Average Yearly Rate
	Incidence/Units	*Rate*	*Incidence/Units*	*Rate*	*Incidence/Units*	*Rate*	*Rate*
57	6/459	13	4/459	9	5.3/459	12	11
70	9/1351	7	27/1351	20	69.3/1351	51	26
83	2/576	3	4/576	7	9.3/576	16	9
134[c]	— —	— —	14/3281	4	25/3281	8	6
145	85/771	110	61/771	79	77.3/771	100	97
166	16/740	22	15/740	20	10.6/740	14	18
196	6/835	7	8/835	10	2.6/835	3	6
256	46/1418	32	51/1418	36	116/1418	82	50
265	25/483	52	15/483	31	25.3/483	52	45
291	2/425	5	8/425	19	16/425	38	20
307	23/376	61	29/376	77	28/376	74	71
315	12/220	55	13/220	59	25.3/220	115	76
447	2/250	8	2/250	8	2.6/250	10	9
505	0/131	0	4/131	31	1.3/131	10	13
622	36/510	71	56/510	110	84/510	165	115
736[c]	— —	— —	23/647	36	24/647	37	36
745[c]	— —	— —	6/132	45	5/132	38	41
775	8/115	70	2/115	17	12/115	104	64

[a]Number of units based on 1970 census statistics.

[b]Boston Police data not available for period October through December 1971. Figures given here are estimated number of incidents and rates extrapolated from October through December.

[c]Suburban police data for 1969 was unavailable.

Table C(2)-4. Residential Burglary Rate per 1000 Households,[a] Non-survey Areas

	1969		*1970*		*1971*[b]		*Average Yearly Rate*
	Incidence/Units	*Rate*	*Incidence/Units*	*Rate*	*Incidence/Units*	*Rate*	
135	102/1385	74	100/1385	72	146.3/1385	106	83
143	6/800	8	6/800	8	13.3/800	17	10
214	0/640	0	4/640	6	5.3/640	8	4
232	2/301	7	1/301	3	4/301	13	7
296	11/342	32	19/342	56	27.6/342	86	56
297	11/301	37	11/301	37	25.3/301	84	52
306	15/313	48	10/313	32	10.6/313	34	38
308	13/279	47	22/279	79	38.6/279	138	88
319	50/815	61	76/815	93	54.6/815	67	73
421	2/549	4	4/549	7	4/549	7	6
467	10/206	49	9/206	44	10.6/206	51	47
470	13/268	49	6/268	22	12/268	45	38
589	2/410	5	5/410	12	73.3/410	179	65
600	5/1038	5	3/1038	3	16/1038	15	7
602	3/846	4	2/846	2	1.3/846	2	2
653	15/126	119	6/126	48	2.6/126	21	62
779	4/305	13	4/305	13	5.3/305	17	14
824	2/643	3	4/643	6	1.3/643	2	3
62	0/1386	0	0/1386	0	0/1386	0	0
530	0/59	0	0/59	0	0/59	0	0
720	2/192	10	1/192	5	2.7/192	14	10

[a] Number of units based on 1970 census statistics.

[b] Boston Police data not available for period October through December 1971. Figures given here are estimated number of incidents and rates extrapolated from October through December.

Table C(2)-5. Average Annual Burglary Rate: RA Compared to Surrounding Neighborhood

RA	RA Residential Rate/1000 DUs	Total[a] Neighborhood Rate/1000 Persons[b]	Neighborhood Residential Rate/ 1000 Persons
57	11	7.0	2.6
83	9	9.4	2.9
134	6	8.7	NA
196	6	9.9	3.5
214	4	9.9	3.5
232	7	4.0	2.0
505	13	8.3	4.9
530	0	4.0	2.6
602	2	9.0	7.2
653	62	8.8	7.1
720	10	6.5	2.3
779	14	9.0	6.1
824	3	6.7	2.5
62	0	23.0	17.5
70	26	23.0	17.5
256	50	24.5	15.5
291	20	17.8	13.7
421	6	14.0	11.0
447	9	16.9	13.0
467	47	14.0	11.0
470	38	14.0	11.0
589	65	11.5	8.9
600	7	11.5	8.9
622	115	20.0	15.5
736	36	11.8	7.1
745	41	11.8	7.1
775	64	13.2	8.9
135	83	59.4	49.8
143	10	28.9	15.0
145	97	28.9	15.0
166	18	32.5	17.7
265	45	33.0	26.6
296	56	33.0	26.6
297	52	34.2	28.0
306	38	31.5	26.7
307	71	31.5	26.7
308	88	34.2	28.0
315	76	31.5	26.7
319	73	31.5	26.7

RAs in Low Rate Neighborhoods (RA 57–824), *RAs in Medium Rate Neighborhoods* (RA 62–775), *RAs in High Rate Neighborhoods* (RA 135–319)

Neighborhood Rate[c]	*Average RA Rate*
Low	8
Medium	28
High	55

[a]Total neighborhood rate includes residential and nonresidential burglaries.

[b]Burglary rates are calculated by 1000 persons rather than dwellings, since the number of nonresidential structures at risk is unknown.

[c]Difference in group rates significant at .05 level.

Table C(2)-6. Average Annual Residential Burglary Rate by Racial Composition of Reporting Areas

White RAs	Rate/1000 Units	Mixed RAs	Rate/1000 Units	Black RAs	Rate/1000 Units
57	11	145	97	265	45
62	0	166	18	296	56
70	26	256	50	297	52
83	9	291	20	306	38
134	6	467	47	307	71
135	83	470	38	308	88
143	10	600	7	315	76
196	6			319	73
214	4			447	9
232	7			589	65
421	6				
505	13				
530	0				
602	2				
622	115				
653	62				
720	10				
736	36				
745	41				
775	64				
779	14				
824	3				

*Average Annual Rate**	
White	19
Mixed	40
Black	59

*Group rates significant at .05 level.

Table C(2)-7.   Average Annual Residential Burglary Rate by Income Level

Lower		*Middle*		*Higher*	
RA	*Rate/1000 DUs*	*RA*	*Rate/1000 DUs*	*RA*	*Rate/1000 DUs*
135	83	57	11	134	6
145	97	62	0	143	10
166	18	70	26	232	7
196	6	83	9	421	6
256	50	214	4	470	38
265	45	306	38	505	13
291	20	307	71	530	0
296	56	308	88	653	62
297	52	315	76	720	10
589	65	319	73	736	36
600	7	467	47	745	41
622	115	447	9		
		602	2		
		775	64		
		779	14		
		824	3		

Income	*Rate**
Lower	47
Middle	27
Higher	13

*Group rates significantly different at .05 level.

Table C(2)-8. Residential Burglary by Percent Population under 18

	%	RA	Average Annual Rate/1000 DUs
	Less than 20%	62	0
		70	26
		135	83
		143	10
		145	97
		602	2
		622	115
		736	36
		745	41
		775	64
	Less than 30%	83	9
		232	7
		291	20
		315	76
		421	6
		470	38
		720	10
		779	14
	Less than 40%	57	11
		134	6
		214	4
		265	45
		296	56
		306	38
		467	47
		505	13
		530	0
		600	7
		653	62
		824	3
		307	71
		308	88
	More than 40%	166	18
		196	6
		256	50
		297	52
		319	73
		447	9
		589	65

*Average Annual Rate/1000 Units**	
Less than 20%	37
Less than 30%	18
Less than 40%	19
Over 40%	41

*Difference between group rates not significant at the .05 level.

Table C(2)-9. Average Annual Residential Burglary Rate by Predominant Housing Type in RA

Single Family	Rate/ 1000 DUs	Small Multi- unit	Rate/ 1000 DUs	Large Multi- unit	Rate/ 1000 DUs	Public Housing	Rate/ 1000 DUs
134	6	57	11	62	0	166	18
470	38	83	9	70	26	196	6
505	13	214	4	135	83	256	50
530	0	232	7	143	10	297	52
653	62	265	45	145	97	306	38
736	36	291	20	307	71	589	65
		296	56	421	6	600	7
		308	88	602	2		
		315	76	622	115		
		319	73	745	41		
		447	9	775	64		
		467	47				
		720	10				
		779	14				
		824	3				

Rate/1000 DUs*	
Single Family	14
Small Multiunit	30
Large Multiunit	37
Public Housing	34

*Difference between group rates not significant at the .05 level.

Table C(2)-10. Regression Results[d]: Percentage Nonwhite

Sample[a]	Constant	Coefficient	R^2	F
Complete (N = 39)	.03 (3.90)[b]	.0004 (2.82)	.16	7.97
Main (N = 28)	*[c]	.0006	.54	32.3
Low Youth (N = 7)	*	*	*	*

[a] Samples explained in text.
[b] Numbers in parentheses are *t* values.
[c] * indicates not significantly different from zero at the .05 level.
[d] The dependent variable in these regressions is residential burglary rate per dwelling unit.

Table C(2)-11. Regression Results:[d] Neighborhood Burglary Rate

Sample[a]	Constant	Coefficient	R^2	F
Complete (N = 39)	*[b]	.0002 (3.96)[c]	.28	15.7
Main (N = 28)	*	.0002 (4.89)	.49	23.9
Low Youth	*	*	*	*

[a] Samples explained in text.
[b] * indicates not significantly different from zero at the .05 level.
[c] Number in parentheses are *t* values.
[d] The dependent variable in these regressions is residential burglary rate per dwelling unit.

Table C(2)-12. RAs in Each Subsample

Main Sample		Low Youth	Suburban
57	308	62	134
83	315	70	720
166	319	135	736
196	421	143	745
214	447	602	
232	467	622	
256	470	775	
265	505		
291	530		
296	589		
297	600		
306	653		
307	779		
	825		

Table C(2)-13. Regression Results:[c] Median Income

Sample[a]	Constant	Coefficient	R^2	F
Complete	.05	−.0002	.05	3.16
(N = 39)	(5.41)[b]	(−1.77)		
	.06	−.004	.06	2.92
(N = 28)	(3.75)	(−1.71)		
Low Youth	.141	−.002	.62	10.7
(N = 7)	(5.27)	(−3.27)		
Suburban	−	.0001	.19	13.8
(N = 4)		(3.03)		

[a]Samples explained in Table C(2)-12.
[b]Numbers in parentheses are *t* values.
[c]The dependent variable in these regressions is residential burglary rate per dwelling unit.

Table C(2)-14. Regression Results:[d] Age

Sample[a]	Constant	Coefficient	R^2	F
Complete	.04	*	*	*
(N = 39)	(3.42)[b]			
Main	*[c]	.03	*	4.83
(N = 28)		(2.20)		

[a]Samples explained in Table C(2)-12.
[b]Numbers in parentheses are *t* values.
[c]* indicates not significantly different from zero at .05 level.
[d]The dependent variable in these regressions is residential burglary rate per dwelling unit.

Table C(2)-15. Regression Results:[d] Housing

Sample[a]	Constant	Coefficient	R^2	F
Complete	.04	*[c]	*	*
(N = 39)	(4.69)[b]			
Main	.03	*	.01	1.04
(N = 28)	(4.21)			
Low Youth	.110	*	.08	1.48
(N = 7)	(2.55)			

[a]Samples explained in text.
[b]Numbers in parentheses are *t* values.
[c]* indicates not significantly different from zero at .05 level.
[d]The dependent variable in these regressions is residential burglary rate per dwelling unit.

Table C(2)—16. Average Annual Residential Burglary Rate by Degree of Social Cohesion[a]

	RA	*Rate/1000 DUs*
Low Cohesion	307	71
	622	116
	745	41
Medium Cohesion	70	26
	134	6
	145	97
	166	18
	196	6
	256	50
	265	45
	291	20
	315	75
	447	9
	736	36
	775	64
High Cohesion	57	11
	83	9
	505	9

Cohesion	*Rate*[b]
Low	90
Medium	28
High	16

[a] Includes only RAs in the household survey.
[b] Differences between groups is not significant at the .05 level.

Table C(2)-17. Percent of Residents Who Called Police in the Last Year

RA Number	% Making a Call
622	65
70	62
736	61
307	57
196	56
145	54
265	54
256	53
775	52
447	49
291	44
505	40
57	37
745	36
166	35
315	23
134	20
83	6

Source: Household Survey.

Table C(2)-18. Average Annual Residential Burglary Rate by Dwelling Occupancy Rates

	RA[a]	*Rate/1,000 DUs*
Low Occupancy	622	116
	745	41
	775	64
Middle Occupancy	57	11
	70	26
	134	6
	145	97
	265	45
	291	20
	307	71
	505	9
	736	36
High Occupancy	83	9
	166	18
	196	6
	256	50
	315	75
	447	9

Occupancy	*Rates*[b]
Low	94
Medium	27
High	28

[a]Includes only RAs in the household survey.
[b]Difference in group rates not significant at the .05 level.

APPENDIX C(3): MAPS

Figure C(3)-1. The Metropolitan Core: City of Boston.

(Numbers Indicate Police Districts)

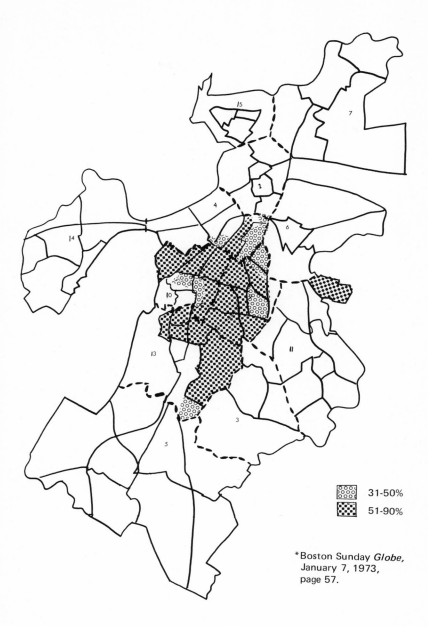

31-50%
51-90%

*Boston Sunday *Globe,*
January 7, 1973,
page 57.

Figure C(3)-2. Blacks as a Percent of Total Population—1970.

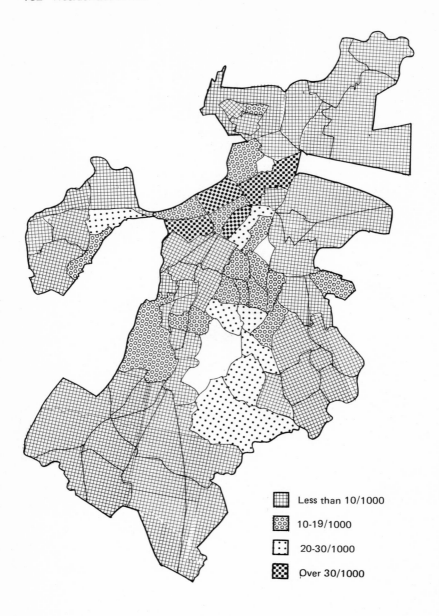

Figure C(3)-3.   Residential Burglaries per **1000** Residents by Neighborhood—1971

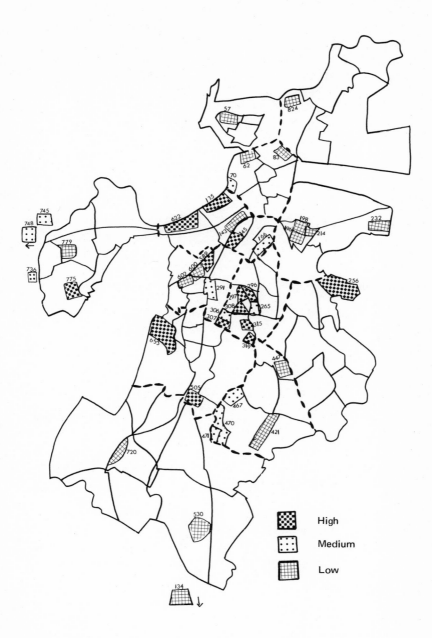

Figure C(3)-4.   Residential Burglary Rate per 1000 Dwelling Units:
Selected RAs, 1969-1971.

   The following maps supplement the discussion in Appendix C(1) of critical factors in the differential distribution of residential burglary rates as exhibited by eight selected RAs. Accompanied by the key below, the maps depict the land use and housing type of each RA and present further information on extent and type of burglary victimization in the area.

Key

Types of burglaries:

    △   daytime, forced

    □   daytime, no force

    ▲   nighttime, forced

    ■   nighttime, no force

  4△   (ex) number of occurences

 Indicates residences where crimes occurred.

 Indicates nonresidential property.

Types of residences:

    D—   dwelling; map notation for a private residential building occupied by not more than two families.

    F—   flat; map notation for a residential building occupied by not more than one family per floor.

    A—   apartments; map notation for a residential building occupied by several families, with at least two per floor.

    R—   rooming; map notation for a residential building containing more than ten rooms used for lodging purposes.

    G—   notation for garages.

Figure C(3)-5. RA 83.

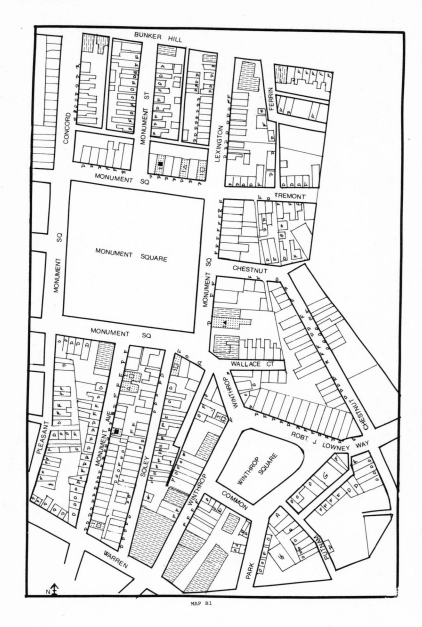

MAP B1

Figure C(3)-6. RA 57.

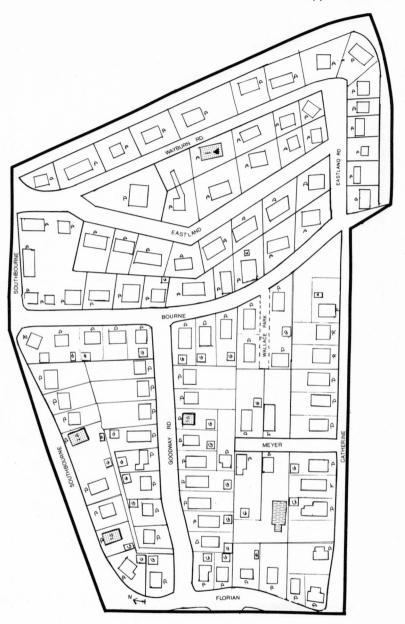

Figure C(3)-7. RA 505.

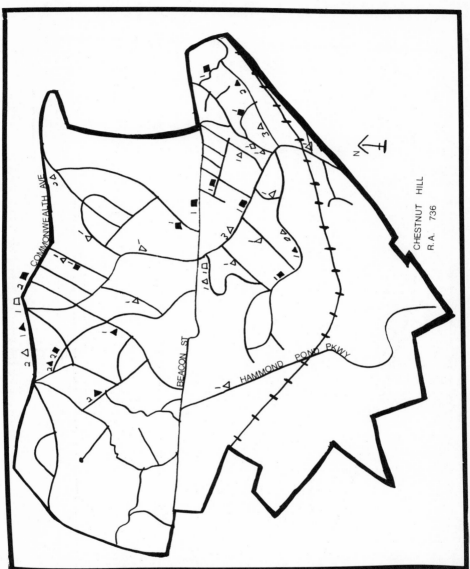

Figure C(3)-8. RA 736.

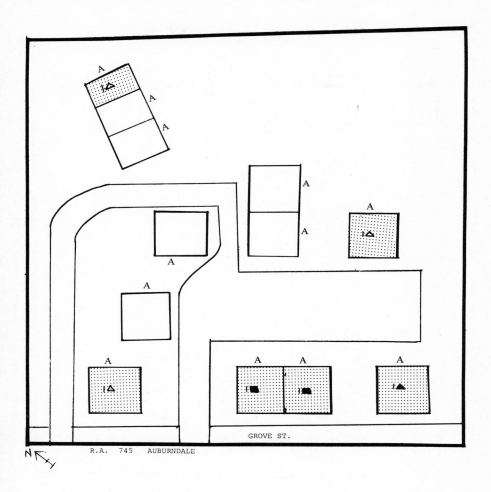

Figure C(3)-9. RA 745—Auburndale.

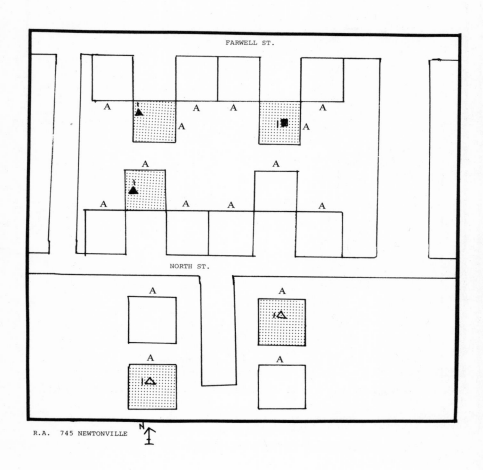

Figure C(3)-10. RA 745—Newtonville.

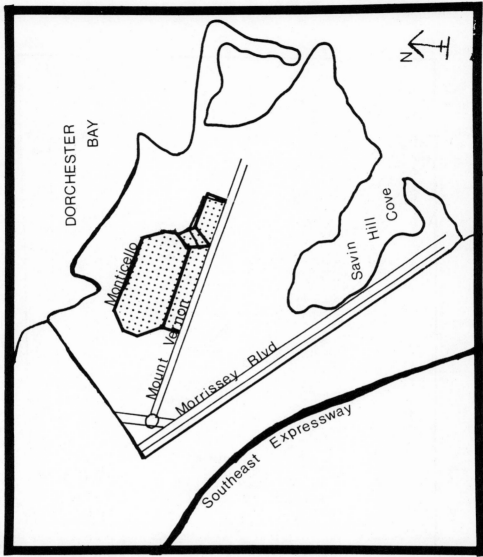

DORCHESTER BAY

Monticello

Mount Vernon

Morrissey Blvd

Savin Hill Cove

Southeast Expressway

N

Figure C(3)-11. RA 256.

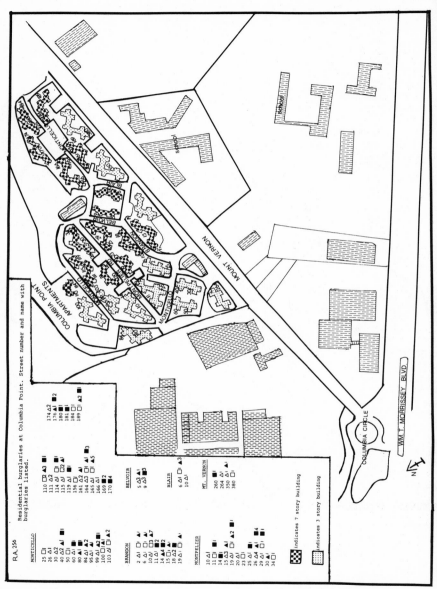

Figure C(3)-12. RA 256.

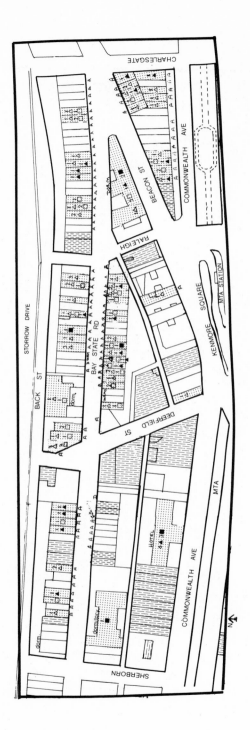

Figure C(3)-13. RA 622.

Figure C(3)-14.   RA315.

APPENDIX D(1): WEIGHTING PROCEDURE

As noted in the text, the victimization and burglary incidence rates in the tables in Chapter 4 and in this Appendix are based on weighted figures to correct for sampling variations. Since households in which a burglary was known to have occurred had a much greater probability of being selected for interviews than other households in an area, and since, also, the probability of random selection of a household would differ from area to area depending on population size, each interview was assigned a "weight" which reflected the probability of selection of that interview. For the interviews with known victims of burglary, the weight was simply the ratio of the number of known victims who could be located to the number of victims interviewed. If, for example, an area had reported 16 burglaries to the police, and from these 16 reports, 8 victims could be located (the others having left the area) and of these 8 victims, four were interviewed, a weight of "2" would be assigned to each interview. For the most part, however, the survey sought to interview all the victims who could be located, so the most common weight assigned to victim interviews was simply "1."

For the random sampling of "nonvictim" households (households which had *not* reported a burglary to the police), the weight assigned to each interview reflects the reciprocal of the sampling fraction of the area in which the household was located. The procedure was as follows: first, an estimate was made (based on the city directory) of the total number of dwelling units in a given area, and the number of known victim units was then subtracted from this number. Probable response and vacancy rates were estimated for each area and from these estimates a sampling interval was established. That is, if 35 interviews were desired for a given area, then it was estimated that 50 names should be included in the sample (anticipating attrition through vacancy and nonresponse). If the total number of nonvictims in the area was 650, then the sampling interval would be 50 out of 650, or 1 in 13. The weight assigned to each random interview would then be 13.

Table D(2)-1. Extent of Multiple Victimization in Low, Middle, and High Crime Rate RAs*

	% of Victims Who Were Victimized More than Once
HC RAs	43%
MC RAs	24
LC RAs	32
Average	28%

*"Crime Rate," in these tables, refers only to the residential burglary rate, and as noted in the text, the victimization rate per thousand is based on weighted frequencies. The number of cases (*n*) refers to the actual number of interviews.

Table D(2)-2. Victimization by Race*

	V. rate	*(n)*	*% Multiply Victimized*
Black	130	(294)	46%
White	110	(604)	22
		(898)	

*Not statistically significant at the .05 level.

Table D(2)-3. Victimization by Race and Income in Low, Middle, and High Crime RAs[a]

HC RAs	V. rate	(n)	Burglary Incidence
Black			
Less than $8,000	80	(87)	120
$8,000-$14,999	180	(30)	180
$15,000 +	230	(20)	370
White			
Less than $8,000	120	(80)	180
$8,000-$14,999	180	(30)	250
$15,000 +	260	(20)	370
MC RAs			
Black			
Less than $8,000	200	(51)	270
$8,000-$14,999	270	(23)	280
$15,000 +	350	(8)	710
White			
Less than $8,000	60	(66)	70
$8,000-$14,999	210	(48)	210
$15,000 +	240	(70)	270
LC RAs			
Black[b]			
Less than $8,000	70	(29)	110
$8,000-$14,999	290	(14)	360
$15,000 +	130	(8)	400
White			
Less than $8,000	80	(110)	130
$8,000-$14,999	50	(75)	50
$15,000 +	110	(33)	110

[a]Statistically significant at the .05 level in high and middle crime RAs only.

[b]Figures for blacks in low crime RAs are based on RAs 196 and 447. If these two RAs are really middle or high crime areas as survey figures suggest, there are no blacks in the low crime RAs.

Table D(2)-4. Age of Head of Household of Those Persons in the Studied RAs Reporting a Burglary to the Police (N = 1526)

Age	Percentage Reporting a Burglary
Under 21 years	10%
21 – 30 years	44
31 – 40 years	16
41 – 50 years	13
51 – 65 years	12
65 + years	5

Table D(2)-5. Victimization by Age and Marital Status of Head of Household*

	V. Rate	(n)
Head to 40 years, not married	440	(147)
Head 40-64 years, not married	390	(69)
Head to 40 years, married (with or without children)	290	(311)
Head 40-64 years, married (with or without children)	270	(198)
Head 65 years +	160	(138)
		(863)

*Statistically significant at the .05 level.

Table D(2)-6. Victimization by Occupation of Head of Household*

	V. Rate	(n)
Professional	430	(179)
Manager	340	(87)
Clerical	350	(112)
Sales	250	(40)
Skilled worker	300	(83)
Semiskilled worker	190	(115)
Service worker	320	(102)
Unskilled	190	(142)

*Not statistically significant at the .05 level.

Table D(2)-7. Victimization by Number of Hours Dwelling Un-occupied on Usual Day*

	V. Rate	*(n)*
None to two hours a day	120	(314)
2 – 7 hours a day	170	(331)
8 or more hours a day	280	(238)
		(883)

*Statistically significant at the .05 level.

Table D(2)-8. Victimization by Social Isolation in Low, Middle, and High Crime RAs*

	V. Rate	*(n)*	*Incidence*	*% Multiply Victimized*
HC RAs				
Isolated	130	(122)	190	46%
Somewhat isolated	70	(115)	120	71
Not isolated	210	(56)	230	10
MC RAs				
Isolated	200	(95)	230	15%
Somewhat isolated	150	(149)	180	20
Not isolated	220	(62)	250	14
LC RAs				
Isolated	100	(72)	170	70%
Somewhat isolated	80	(139)	100	25
Not isolated	30	(92)	40	33
		(902)		

*Statistically significant at the .05 level in low crime RAs only.

Table D(2)-9. Household Protective Measures*

	Special Locks	Alarms	Weapons	Wire Mesh or Bars	Patrolman	Other	NA	Nothing
Victims	63	3	17	3	*	19	*	18
Non-victims	48	2	10	*	7	16	*	36
% of sample	50	3	11	*	6	17	*	33

*Here is a list of some things people have to protect their homes. Which of the things on the list do you (and your family) have? (Anything not on the list?)

Table D(2)-10. Burglary Incidence Rate Through Door by Door Vulnerability and Income of Household

	Nonstandard Doors		All Standard Doors	
Income	Rate	(n)	Rate	(n)
All RAs				
Less than $8,000	72	(394)	47	(35)
$8,000-$15,000	62	(211)	0	(11)
More than $15,000	134	(145)	0	(16)

Table D(2)-11. Burglary Incidence Rate Through Door by Door Vulnerability and Number of Hours Unoccupied per Week

	Nonstandard Doors		All Standard Doors	
Occupancy	Rate	(n)	Rate	(n)
All RAs				
Less than 5	50	(348)	54	(19)
5 – 35	79	(241)	5	(18)
More than 35	113	(212)	0	(13)

APPENDIX E: TABLES

Table E-1. What Effect Do the Following Detection and Access Deterrents Have on Interviewees' Decision to Hit a Residence, in Total, and by Age, Race, and Drug Use?

		Age			Race		Drug Use	
	Total	*Under 18*	*18-25*	*Over 25*	*W*	*Non W*	*DU*	*Non DU*
Full-time occupant								
Would prevent offense	67%	68%	63%	74%	75%	57%	60%	73%
Might prevent offense	21	16	23	22	15	29	24	18
No effect	12	16	15	4	10	14	16	9
Total number answering	90	19	48	23	48	42	45	45
Neighbors checking								
Would prevent offense	23%	25%	14%	35%	24%	21%	25%	21%
Might prevent offense	39	44	35	41	46	31	32	44
No effect	39	31	52	24	30	48	43	35
Total number answering	62	16	29	17	33	29	28	34
Police security patrols								
Would prevent offense	14%	26%	7%	18%	4%	25%	10%	18%
Might prevent offense	37	42	38	32	48	25	39	36
No effect	49	32	56	50	48	50	51	47
Total number answering	86	19	45	22	46	40	41	45
Evidence of alarm								
Would prevent offense	36%	47%	38%	25%	37%	35%	41%	31%
Might prevent offense	37	24	33	54	40	35	36	38
No effect	27	29	29	21	23	30	23	31
Total number answering	86	17	45	24	43	43	44	42

Deterrents—Detection

Table E-1. (cont.)

			Age			Race		Drug Use	
		Total	Under 18	18-25	Over 25	W	Non W	DU	Non DU
Detection	**Good lighting** Would prevent offense	9%	7%	9%	11%	13%	4%	3%	16%
	Might prevent offense	24	29	12	42	36	7	17	32
	No effect	67	64	79	47	51	89	80	52
	Total number answering	66	14	33	19	39	27	35	31
Access	**Strong locks** Would prevent offense	5%	7%	4%	5%	5%	5%	7%	2%
	Might prevent offense	33	33	29	40	24	42	31	34
	No effect*	63	61	67	55	71	54	62	63
	Total number answering	83	18	45	20	42	41	42	41
	Steel doors and frames Would prevent offense	5%	25%	16%	16%	18%	18%	23%	12%
	Might prevent offense	45	38	32	53	39	39	39	39
	No effect	50	38	51	32	44	42	39	49
	Total number answering	62	16	37	19	39	33	39	33
Detection & Access	**Dog** Would prevent offense	22%	24%	24%	14%	24%	19%	19%	24%
	Might prevent offense	39	33	31	64	38	41	45	33
	No effect	39	43	45	23	38	41	36	42
	Total number answering	92	21	49	22	50	42	47	45

(Left margin label spanning rows: Deterrents (cont.))

*Two different answers here:
1. "I haven't found a lock I can't get through yet." or
2. "Just go through the window."

Bibliography

NATURE OF RESIDENTIAL CRIME

Conklin, John. *Robbery and the Criminal Justice System*. Philadelphia: J.B. Lippincott Co., 1972.

Federal Bureau of Investigation. *Uniform Crime Reports*. Washington: U.S. Government Printing Office.

Glaser, Daniel, ed. *Crime in the City*. New York: Harper and Row, 1970.

Martin, John M. *Juvenile Vandalism, A Study of Its Nature and Prevention*. Springfield, Illinois: Charles C. Thomas, 1961.

Report of the President's Commission on Crime in the District of Columbia. Washington: U.S. Government Printing Office, 1966.

Sagalyn, Arnold. *The Crime of Robbery in the United States*. Washington: U.S. Government Printing Office, 1971.

Scarr, Harry A. *Patterns of Burglary*. National Institute of Law Enforcement and Criminal Justice. Washington: U.S. Government Printing Office, 1972.

Shover, Neal Elwood. *Burglary as an Occupation*. Ph.D. Dissertation, University of Illinois at Urbana-Champaign, 1971.

Wilson, James Q. "Crime in the Street." *The Public Interest* 5 (Fall 1966): 26-35.

Wolfgang, Marvin E. *Patterns of Criminal Homicide*. Philadelphia: University of Pennsylvania Press, 1958.

EXTENT AND CONSEQUENCES OF RESIDENTIAL CRIME

Biderman, Albert D. "Social Indicators and Goals." *Social Indicators*. Cambridge, Massachusetts: M.I.T. Press, 1966.

153

Cardarelli, Albert P. *Crime in Boston: An Analysis of Serious Crime Patterns within 81 Neighborhoods.* Mayor's Office of Justice Administration. Boston, 1971.

Cutler, Stepehen and Albert J. Reiss, Jr. "Crimes Against Public and Quasi-Public Organizations in Boston, Chicago, and Washington, D.C." (A special survey for the President's Commission on Law Enforcement and Administration of Justice, 1966.)

Ennis, Philip H. *Criminal Victimization in the United States: A Report of a National Survey.* Washington: U.S. Government Printing Office, 1967.

Ferdinand, Theodore N. "The Criminal Patterns of Boston Since 1840." *American Journal of Sociology* 73 (1967): 84-99.

Loth, David. *Crime in the Suburbs.* New York: William Morrow and Co., 1967.

National Commission on the Causes and Prevention of Violence. Task Force on Individual Acts of Violence, "Levels and Trends of Individual Violence in the United States." *Crimes of Violence.* Washington: U.S. Government Printing Office, 1970, Chapter 3.

Normandeau, Andre. *Trends and Patterns in Crimes of Robbery.* Ph.D. Dissertation, University of Pennsylvania, 1968.

President's Commission on Crime in the District of Columbia, *Report.* Washington: U.S. Government Printing Office, 1966.

President's Commission on Law Enforcement and Administration of Justice. *Task Force Report: Crime and Its Impact: An Assessment.* Washington: U.S. Government Printing Office, 1967.

Reiss, Albert J. and Donald J. Black. *Studies in Crime and Law Enforcement in Major Metropolitan Areas.* Vols. I and II. Washington: U.S. Government Printing Office, 1967.

Sagi, Phillip C. and Charles F. Wellford. "Age Composition and Patterns of Change in Criminal Statistics." *Journal of Criminal Law, Criminology and Police Science* 59 (1968): 29-36.

Schafer, Stephen. *The Victim and His Criminal: A Study in Functional Responsibility.* New York: Random House, 1968.

Short, James F. and S. Ivan Nye. "Extent of Unrecorded Delinquency: Tentative Conclusions." *Journal of Criminal Law, Criminology and Police Science* 49 (November-December 1958): 296-302.

BEHAVIOR OF OFFENDERS

Barnes, Robert Earl. *Are You Safe from Burglars?* Garden City, New York: Doubleday, Inc., 1971.

Becker, Howard S., ed. *The Other Side: Perspectives on Deviance.* New York: MacMillan, 1964.

Bloch, Herbert A. and Gilbert Geis. *Man, Crime and Society: The Forms of Criminal Behavior.* New York: Random House, Inc., 1962.

Bowers, John. "Big City Theives." *Harper's Magazine* 234 (February 1967): 50-54.

Chapman, Dennis. *Sociology and the Stereotype of the Criminal.* Tavistock
    Publications, 1968.
Clinard, Marshall B. *Sociology of Deviant Behavior.* 3rd ed. New York: Holt,
    Rinehart and Winston, 1968.
Clinard, Marshall B. and Richard Quinney. *Criminal Behavior Systems: A Typology.* New York: Holt, Rinehart and Winston, 1967.
Gibbons, Don C. *Changing the Lawbreaker.* New Jersey: Prentice-Hall, 1965.
Gibbons, Don C. *Society, Crime and Criminal Careers.* New Jersey: Prentice-Hall, 1968.
Gibbons, Don C. and Donald L. Garrity. "Definition and Analysis of Certain
    Criminal Types." *Journal of Criminal Law, Criminology and Police
    Science* 53 (1962): 27-35.
Goodman, Leonard H., Trudy Miller and Paul DeForrest. *A Study of the Deterrent Value of Crime Prevention Measures as Perceived by Criminal
    Offenders.* Washington: Bureau of Social Science Research, 1966.
Irwin, John. *The Felon.* Englewood Cliffs, New Jersey: Prentice-Hall, 1970.
Martin, John Bartlow. *My Life in Crime: The Autobiography of a Professional
    Criminal, Reported by the Author.* New York: Harper Bros., 1952.
Miller, Walter B. "Theft Behavior in City Gangs," in Malcolm W. Klein, ed.,
    Juvenile Gangs in Context. Englewood Cliffs, New Jersey: Prentice-Hall, 1967.
National Commission on the Causes and Prevention of Violence, "Recidivism
    Over the Criminal Career." *Crimes of Violence.* National Commission
    on the Causes and Prevention of Violence Staff Study Series, Vol.
    12. Washington: U.S. Government Printing Office, 1970.
President's Commission on Law Enforcement and Administration of Justice.
    Task Force Report: Crime and Its Impact: An Assessment. Washington: U.S. Government Printing Office, 1967. Chapter 7, "Professional Crime."
Roebuck, Julian B. "A Criticism of Gibbons' and Garrity's Criminal Typology."
    Journal of Criminal Law, Criminology, and Police Science 54
    (December 1963): 476-478.
Roebuck, Julian B. *Criminal Typology.* Springfield, Illinois: Charles C. Thomas,
    1967.
Roebuck, Julian B. and Ronald Johnson. "The Jack-of-all-Trades Offender."
    Crime and Delinquency 8 (April 1962).
Short, James F., ed. *Law and Order: Modern Criminals,* 1970.
Shover, Neal E. *Burglary as an Occupation.* Ph.D. Dissertation, University of
    Michigan. Ann Arbor, Michigan: University Microfilms, 1971.
Sutherland, Edwin. *The Professional Thief.* Chicago: University of Chicago
    Press, 1937.

LIFE HISTORY OF OFFENDERS

Barnes, Robert E. *Are You Safe from Burglars?* Garden City, New York: Doubleday and Co., 1971.

Carter, Thomas. "How I'd Rob Your House." *Life* 43 (May 31, 1966): 29.
Haveman, E. "History of a Burglar." *Life* 43 (October 7, 1957): 147-151.
Jackson, Bruce. *A Thief's Primer.* New York: The MacMillan Co., 1969.
McKelway, St. Clair. "The Burglar with the Notebooks," in *The Big Little Man from Brooklyn.* Boston: Houghton Mifflin Co., 1969.
Malcolm X. *Autobiography of Malcolm X.* New York: Grove Press, 1964.
Williamson, Henry. *Hustler!* New York: Doubleday and Co., 1968.

FACTORS AND THEORIES

Clark, John P. and Eugene P. Wenninger. "Socio-Economic Class and Area as Correlates of Illegal Behavior Among Juveniles." *American Sociological Review* 27 (1962): 826-834.
Clinard, Marshall B. *Sociology of Deviant Behavior.* Revised edition. New York: Holt, Rinehart and Winston, 1963.
Cloward, Richard A. and Lloyd E. Ohlin. *Delinquency and Opportunity.* Glencoe, Illinois: The Free Press, 1960.
Cohen, Albert K. *Delinquent Boys.* Glencoe, Illinois: The Free Press, 1955.
Durkheim, Emile. *Rules of the Sociological Method.* 8th edition. Sarah A. Solway and John H. Mueller, trans., and George E.G. Catlin, ed. Glencoe, Illinois: The Free Press, 1950.
Falk, Gerhard J. "The Influence of Season on the Crime Rate." *Journal of Criminal Law, Criminology and Police Science* 43 (1952): 199-213.
Ferdinand, Theodore. "The Offense Patterns and Family Structures of Urban, Village and Rural Delinquency." *Journal of Criminal Law, Criminology and Police Science* 55 (1964): 86-93.
Fooner, Michael. "Money and Economic Factors in Crime and Delinquency." *Criminology* 8 (1971): 311-332.
Glueck, Sheldon and Eleanor Glueck. *Juvenile Delinquents Grow Up.* Cambridge: Harvard University Press, 1940.
Kobrin, Solomon. "The Conflict of Values in Delinquency Areas." *American Sociological Review* 16 (October 1951): 653-661.
Lander, Bernard. *Toward an Understanding of Juvenile Delinquency.* New York: Columbia University Press, 1954.
Matza, David. *Becoming Deviant.* Englewood Cliffs, New Jersey: Prentice-Hall, 1969.
Matza, David. *Delinquency and Drift.* New York: John Wiley and Sons, Inc., 1964.
McCord, William and Joan McCord, with Irving Kenneth Zola, *Origins of Crime: A New Evaluation of the Cambridge-Somerville Youth Study.* New York: Columbia University Press, 1959.
Merton, Robert K. "Social Structure and Anomie." *American Sociological Review* 3 (October 1938): 672-682.
Merton, Robert K. *Social Theory and Social Structure.* New York: The Free Press of Glencoe, 1957.
Miller, Walter B. "Lower Class Culture as a Generating Milieu of Gang Delinquency." *The Journal of Social Issues* 14 (1958): 5-19.

Moses, Earl R. "Differentials in Crime Rate between Negroes and Whites."
    American Sociological Review 12 (August 1947): 411-420.
Ohlin, Lloyd E. "The Effect of Social Change on Crime and Law Enforcement."
    Notre Dame Lawyer 43 (1968): 834-846.
Reckless, Walter C. *The Crime Problem.* 3rd edition. New York: Appleton-
    Century-Crofts, Inc., 1961.
Shaw, Clifford R. and Henry E. McKay. *Juvenile Delinquency and Urban Areas.*
    Chicago: University of Chicago Press, 1942.
Spergel, Irving. *Racketville, Slumtown, Haulberg: An Exploratory Study of
    Delinquent Subcultures.* Chicago: University of Chicago Press, 1964.
Sykes, Gresham M. and David Matza. "Techniques of Neutralization: A Theory
    of Delinquency." *American Sociological Review* 22 (December
    1957): 664-670.
Taft, Donald R. "Testing the Selective Influence of Areas of Delinquency."
    American Journal of Sociology 38 (March 1933): 699-712.
Thrasher, Frederick M. *The Gang.* Chicago: University of Chicago Press, 1927.
Willie, C.V. and A. Gershenovitz. "Juvenile Delinquency in Racially Mixed
    Areas." *American Sociological Review* 29 (October 1964): 740-744.
Willie, Charles V. "The Relative Contribution of Family Status and Economic
    Status to Juvenile Delinquency." *Social Problems* 14:3 (Winter
    1967): 326-335.
Wilson, James Q. "A Reader's Guide to the Crime Commission Reports." *The
    Public Interest* 9 (Fall 1967): 64-82.

DRUGS

Ball, John. "Two Patterns of Narcotic Drug Addiction in the United States."
    Journal of Criminal Law, Criminology and Police Science 56:1
    (1965): 203-211.
Blum, Richard. "Drugs and Violence," in the National Commission on the
    Causes and Prevention of Violence, Task Force on Individual Acts
    of Violence, *Crimes of Violence.* National Commission on the
    Causes and Prevention of Violence Staff Study Series, Vol. 13.
    Washington: U.S. Government Printing Office, 1970.
Blum, Richard. "Mind-altering Drugs and Dangerous Behavior: Alcohol," in
    the President's Commission on Law Enforcement and the Admin-
    istration of Justice, *Task Force Report: Drunkenness.* Washington:
    U.S. Government Printing Office, 1967.
Blum, Richard. "Mind-altering Drugs and Dangerous Behavior: Narcotics," in
    the President's Commission on Law Enforcement and the Admin-
    istration of Justice, *Task Force Report: Narcotics and Drug Abuse.*
    Washington: U.S. Government Printing Office, 1967.
Chein, Isidor, Donald L. Gerald, Robert S. Lee and Eva Rosenfeld. *The Road
    to H: Narcotics, Delinquency and Social Policy.* New York: Basic
    Books, Inc., 1964.
Chein, Isidor and Eva Rosenfeld. "Juvenile Narcotics Use." *Law and Contem-
    porary Problems* 22 (1957): 52-68.

Finestone, Harold. "Narcotics and Criminality." *Law and Contemporary Problems* 22 (1957): 69-85.

Kolb, Lawrence. Drug Addiction: *A Medical Problem.* Springfield, Illinois: Charles C. Thomas, 1962).

Larner, Jeremy and Ralph Tefferteller. *The Addict in the Street.* New York: Grove Press, Inc., 1964.

Mauere, David W. and Victor H. Vogel. *Narcotics and Narcotic Addiction.* Springfield, Illinois: Charles C. Thomas, 1967.

Morgan, James. "Drug Addiction: Criminal or Medical Problem?" *Police* 9 (1955).

New York City Police Department, Statistical and Records Bureau. *Statistical Report of Narcotic Arrests and Arrests of Narcotic Users,* 1968-1969. New York: New York City Police Department, no date.

O'Donnell, John A. "Narcotic Addiction and Crime." *Social Problems* 13 (1966): 374-384.

President's Commission on Law Enforcement and Administration of Justice, Task Force on Narcotics and Drug Abuse. *Task Force Report: Narcotics and Drug Abuse.* Washington: U.S. Government Printing Office, 1967.

U.S. Congress, Senate Committee on the District of Columbia, *Crime in the National Capital.* Hearings on Drug Abuse in the Washington Area. 91st Congress, 1st Session. Washington: U.S. Government Printing Office, 1969.

Roebuck, Julian. "The Negro Addict as an Offender Type." *Journal of Criminal Law, Criminology and Police Science* 53 (1962): 36-43.

Singer, Max. "The Vitality of Mythical Numbers." *Public Interest* 23 (Spring 1971): 3-9.

Straus, Nathan, II, ed. *Addicts and Drug Abuse: Current Approaches to the Problem.* New York: Twayne Publishers, Inc., 1971.

Sutter, Alan. "The Righteous Dope Fiend." *Issues in Criminology* 2:2 (Fall, 1966): 200-213. Reprinted in Marvin E. Wolfgang, Leonard Savitz and Norman Johnson, eds., *The Sociology of Crime and Delinquency,* 2nd edition. New York: John Wiley and Sons, Inc., 1970.

Williams, John B., ed. *Narcotics.* Dubuque, Iowa: William C. Brown Co., 1963.

Wilson, James Q., Mark H. Moore, and I. David Wheat, Jr. "The Problem of Heroin." *The Public Interest* 29 (Fall 1972): 3-28.

Winick, Charles. "Drug Addiction and Crime." *Current History* 52 (June 1967): 349-353.

Yurick, Sol. "The Political Economy of Junk." *Monthly Review* (December 1970): 22-37.

ECOLOGY

Boggs, Sarah L. *The Ecology of Crime Occurrence in St. Louis: A Reconceptualization of Crime Rates and Patterns.* Ph.D. Dissertation, Washington University, 1964.

Hawley, Amos H. *Urban Society: An Ecological Approach.* New York: The Ronald Press Co., 1971.

Mays, J.B. "Crime and the Urban Pattern." *Sociological Review* 16 (July 1968): 241-255.

Morris, Terrance. *The Criminal Area: A Study in Social Ecology.* New York: Humanities Press, 1958.

Normandeau, A. and B. Schwartz. "A Crime Classification of American Metropolitan Areas." *Criminology* 9 (1970): 228-247.

Polk, Kenneth. "Urban Social Areas and Delinquency." *Social Problems* 14:3 (Winter 1967): 320-325.

Quinney, Richard. "Crime, Delinquency, and Social Areas." *Journal of Research in Crime and Delinquency* 1 (1964): 149-154.

Quinney, Richard. "Structural Characteristics, Population Areas, and Crime Rates in the United States." *Journal of Criminal Law, Criminology, and Police Science* 57 (March 1966): 45-52.

Schmid, Calvin. "Urban Crime Areas: Part I." *American Sociological Review* 25 (August 1960)? "Urban Crime Areas: Part II." *American Sociological Review* 25 (October 1960).

Schuessler, Karl. "Components of Variations in City Crime Rates." *Social Problems* 9 (1962): 314-323.

Turner, Stanley. "The Ecology of Delinquency." In Thorsten Sellin and Marvin Wolfgang, eds., *Delinquency: Selected Studies.* New York: John Wiley and Sons, Inc., 1969.

Wilkes, Judith A. "Ecological Correlates of Crime and Delinquency." In the President's Commission on Law Enforcement and Administration of Justice. *Task Force Report: Crime and Its Impact— An Assessment.* Washington: U.S. Government Printing Office, 1967.

POLICE AND SECURITY

Biderman, Albert D., Louise A. Johnson, Jennie McIntyre, and Adrienne Weir. *Report on a Pilot Study in the District of Columbia on Victimization and Attitudes Toward Law Enforcement.* The President's Commission on Law Enforcement and Administration of Justice. Field Surveys I. Washington: U.S. Government Printing Office, 1967.

Boston, City of. Mayor's Committee for the Administration of Justice. *Challenging Crime.* Boston: City of Boston, 1970.

Campbell, James. S., Joseph R. Sahid and David P. Stang. *Law and Order Reconsidered: A Staff Report to the National Commission on the Causes and Prevention of Violence.* New York: Bantam Books, 1970.

Chapman, Samuel G. *Police Patrol Readings.* Springfield, Illinois: Charles C. Thomas, 1970.

Chicago Police Department, Operations Research Task Force, *Allocation of Resources in the Chicago Police Force* (November 1969).

Church, Orin. "Crime Prevention: A Stitch in Time." *Police Chief* (March 1970): 52-54.

Clift, Raymond. *A Guide to Modern Police Thinking.* Cincinnati: W. Anderson Co., 1956.

"Crime Prevention—Part 2." *The Police Chief* 34 (June 1967): 10-24.

Eastman, George, ed. *Municipal Police Administration.* 7th edition. Washington: ICMA, 1971.

Elliott, J.F. and Thomas J. Sardino. "The Time Required to Commit A Crime." *Police* 16:4 (1971): 26-29.

The Functions of the Police in Modern Society, PHS No. 2059. Washington: U.S. Government Printing Office.

Greenwood, Peter W. *An Analysis of the Apprehension Activities of the New York City Police Department.* New York: Rand Institute, 1970.

Klotter, John C. and Robert I. Cusick, Jr. *Burglary: Prevention, Investigation and Prosecution.* Louisville, Kentucky: University of Louisville (no date).

President's Commission on Law Enforcement and Administration of Justice, *Task Force Report: Science and Technology.* Washington: U.S. Government Printing Office, 1967.

Press, S. James. *Some Effects of an Increase in Police Manpower in the Twentieth Precinct of New York City.* New York: Rand Institute, 1971.

Private Police in the U.S.: Findings and Recommendations. Vol. 1, R-869, U.S. Department of Justice.

The Private Police Industry: Its Nature and Extent. Vol. 2, R-870, U.S. Department of Justice.

Reiss, Albert J., Jr. *The Police and the Public.* New Haven: Yale University Press, 1971.

Smith, Bruce. *Police Systems in the United States.* New York: Harper and Row, 1960.

Standards for Burglary Prevention. McLean, Virginia: Research Analysis Corporation, September 1971.

Webster, John A. "Police Task and Time Study." *Journal of Criminal Law, Criminology and Police Science* (March 1970): 94-102.

Wilson, James Q. "Crime and Law Enforcement." *Agenda for the Nation,* Kermit Gordon, ed. Washington: Brookings Institution.

Wilson, James Q. *Varieties of Police Behavior.* Cambridge: Harvard University Press, 1968.

Wilson, O.W. and Roy C. McLaren. *Police Administration.* 3rd edition. New York: McGraw Hill, 1972.

CITIZEN PATROLS AND CITIZEN BEHAVIOR

Marx, Gary T. and Dane Archer. "Citizen Involvement in the Law Enforcement Process." *American Behavioral Scientist* 15:1 (1971): 52-72.

Marx, Gary T. and Dane Archer. *Picking Up the Gun: Some Organizational and Survey Data on Community Police Patrols.* Cambridge: M.I.T.-Harvard Joint Center for Urban Studies, 1972.

McIntrye, Jennie. "Public Attitudes Toward Crime and Law Enforcement." *Annals of the American Academy of Political and Social Science.* (November 1967).

Nash, George. *The Community Patrol Corps: A Description and Evaluation of a One-Week Experiment.* New York: Columbia University, Bureau of Applied Social Research, 1968.

Nelson, Harold A. "The Defenders: A Case Study of an Informal Police Organization." *Social Problems* 15:2 (Fall 1967).

PHYSICAL DESIGN

Angel, Shlomo. *Discouraging Crime Through City Planning.* Working Paper #75. Berkeley: University of California, 1968.

Fairley, W., M.I. Liechenstein and A. Westin. *Improving Public Safety in Urban Apartment Dwellings: Security Concepts and Experimental Design for New York City Housing Authority Buildings.* New York: Rand Institute, June 1971.

Jacobs, Jane. *The Death and Life of Great American Cities.* New York: Random House, 1961.

Liechenstein, Michael I. *Design for Security.* New York: Rand Institute, April 1971.

Liechenstein, Michael I. *Reducing Crime in Apartment Dwellings: A Methodology for Comparing Security Alternatives.* New York: Rand Institute (June 1971).

Luedtke, Gerald and Associates, *Crime and the Physical City.* Detroit: by the author, 1972.

Newman, Oscar. *Defensible Space: Design for the Improvement of Security in Urban Residential Areas.* New York: MacMillan, 1972.

President's Commission on Law Enforcement and Administration of Justice. *Task Force Report: Science and Technology.* Washington: U.S. Government Printing Office, 1967.

Rainwater, Lee. "The Lessons of Pruitt-Igoe." *The Public Interest* 8 (Summer 1967): 116-126.

HOME PROTECTION

Alexander, George. "A Nervous New Yorker's Guide to Safety Devices." *New York Magazine.*

"Burglarproofing Your Home." *Mechanics Illustrated* (July 1970).

Burns, D.B. "How to Protect Your Valuables from Burglars." *Popular Science Monthly* 191 (September 1967): 80-83.

Carmen, John and Byron Fielding. "Safety and Security in Multi-Family Housing Complexes." *Journal of Housing* 28 (June 6, 1971): 277-281.

Chleboun, T. P. and K.M. Duvall. *An Evaluation of Small Business and Residential Alarm Systems.* GTE Sylvania, Inc., Security Systems Department, Vol. 1, J-LEAA, 003-72, June 1972.

DeCelle, Jack. *The Safety Strategy: How to Keep Crime From Happening to You!* Joseph Rank Publishers, 1971.

Ellison, Bob and Jill Shipstad. *This Book Can Save Your Life!* New York: New American Library, 1968.

Furlong, William Barry. "How to Keep Thieves Out of Your Home." *Good Housekeeping* 167 (July 1968): 63-69.

Galub, Jack. "Burglars Will Get You If You Don't Watch Out." *American Home* 73 (September 1970): 103.

Gavzer, Bernard. *On Guard: Protect Yourself Against the Criminal.* New York: The Associated Press, 1970.

Hair, Robert A. and Samm Sinclair Baker. *How to Protect Yourself Today.* New York: Stein and Day, 1970.

Hamilton, Mildred. "So You Think You're Insurable." *San Francisco Examiner* (April 18, 1972): 19.

Holcomb, Richard L. *Protection Against Burglary.* Iowa City, Iowa: University of Iowa, 1953.

Hunter, George. *How to Defend Yourself, Your Family and Your Home.* New York: McKay, 1967.

Kaufman, Ulrich. *How to Avoid Burglary, Housebreaking and Other Crimes.* New York: Crown Publishers, Inc., 1967.

Moolman, Val. *Practical Ways to Prevent Burglary and Illegal Entry.* New York: Cornerstone Library, 1970.

Standards for Burglary Prevention. McLean, Virginia: Research Analysis Corporation, September 1971.

Worsnop, Richard L. "Burglary Prevention." *Editorial Research Reports* (January 17, 1968): 43-60.

MISCELLANEOUS

Bauer, Raymond A., ed. *Social Indicators.* Cambridge: M.I.T. Press, 1967.

Cavan, Ruth Shonle. *Criminology.* 3rd edition. New York: Thomas Y. Crowell Co., 1962.

Clark, Ramsey. *Crime in America.* New York: Simon and Schuster, Inc., 1970.

Giallambardo, Rose, ed. *Juvenile Delinquency.* New York: John Wiley and Sons, Inc., 1966.

Glaser, Daniel. *Adult Crime and Social Policy.* Englewood Cliffs, New Jersey: Prentice-Hall, 1972.

Lewin, Stephen, ed. *Crime and Its Prevention.* New York: H.W. Wilson Co., 1968.

McLennan, Barbara N. and Kenneth McLennan. "Public Policy and the Control of Crime." *Crime in Urban Society.* New York: Dunellen Publishing Co., 1970.

Morris, Norval and Gordon Hawkins. *The Honest Politician's Guide to Crime Control.* Chicago: University of Chicago Press, 1970.

President's Commission on Law Enforcement and Administration of Justice. *The Challenge of Crime in a Free Society.* Washington: U.S. Government Printing Office, 1967.

Wolfgang, Marvin, Leonard Savitz and Norman Johnson. *The Sociology of Crime and Delinquency.* Second edition. New York: John Wiley & Sons, Inc., 1970.

About the Author

Thomas A. Reppetto is presently an associate professor of criminal justice at the John Jay College of Criminal Justice of the City University of New York. From 1952 to 1967 he was a member of the Chicago police department, rising from patrolman to commander of detectives.

Professor Reppetto holds a Doctoral degree in public administration from the John F. Kennedy School of Government at Harvard University.

Professor Reppetto has served as a research associate at the MIT-Harvard Joint Center for Urban Studies and as a consultant or advisor to various governmental and private organizations including the Department of Justice, HUD, New England Governors Conference, City of Boston, and the Ford Foundation. He is the author of several papers as well as longer studies on various aspects of the criminal justice system.

Thomas A. Reppetto is presently an associate professor of criminal justice at the
John Jay College of Criminal Justice of the
City University of New York. From 1952
to 1967 he was a member of the Chicago
police department, rising from patrolman
to commander of detectives. Professor
Reppetto holds a doctorate in public administration from the John F. Kennedy School
of Government, Harvard University. He has
served as a research associate at the M.I.T.-
Harvard Joint Center for Urban Studies and
as a consultant or advisor to various governmental and private organizations including
the Department of Justice, HUD, New
England Governors' Conference, City of
Boston, and the Ford Foundation. He is
the author of several papers as well as longer
studies on various aspects of the criminal
justice system.